APPROVAL ADDICTION

Overcoming Your Need to Please·Everyone

JOYCE MEYER

NEW YORK   BOSTON   NASHVILLE

Unless otherwise indicated, Scriptures are taken from the Amplified® Bible. Copyright © 1954, 1962, 1965, 1987 by The Lockman Foundation. Used by permission.

Scripture quotations marked KJV are taken from the King James Version of the Bible.

Scripture quotations marked "MESSAGE" are taken from The Message: The Bible in Contemporary Language [MESSAGE] by Eugene H. Peterson. Copyright © 2002 by Eugene H. Peterson. NavPress, P.O. Box 35001, Colorado Springs, CO 80935. Used by permission.

Scripture quotations marked NIV are taken from The Holy Bible, New International Version®. Copyright © 1973, 1978, 1984 by the International Bible Society. All rights reserved.

Scripture quotations marked NKJV are taken from the New King James Version. Copyright © 1982 by Thomas Nelson, Inc. Used by permission. All rights reserved.

FaithWords
Hachette Book Group
1290 Avenue of the Americas
New York, NY 10104

Visit our website at www.faithwords.com

Printed in the United States of America

Originally published in hardcover by Hachette Book Group.

First Trade Edition: November 2008

10   9   8   7

FaithWords is a division of Hachette Book Group, Inc.
The FaithWords name and logo are trademarks of
Hachette Book Group, Inc.

The Library of Congress has cataloged the hardcover edition as follows:

Meyer, Joyce.
Approval addition : overcoming your need to please everyone / Joyce Meyer.
    p. cm.
    Summary: "Author tackles a lack of self-esteem and the need to please others as a major problem in relationships and offers guidance via Christian belief and values" —Provided by the publisher.
    ISBN 0-446-57772-3 — ISBN 0-446-57852-5 (large print)
    1. Self-esteem—Religious aspects—Christianity.   2. Assertiveness (Psychology)—Religious aspects—Christianity.   3. Interpersonal relations—Religious aspects—Christianity.   I. Title.
BV4598.24.M49 2005
248.4—dc22   2004026205

ISBN 978-0-446-50490-4 (pbk.)

Contents

Understanding Approval Addiction

There is an epidemic of insecurity in our society today. Many people are insecure and feel bad about themselves, which steals their joy and causes major problems in all their relationships.

I know the effect insecurity can have on lives because I experienced it myself. I know what it does to a person. Those who have been hurt badly through abuse or severe rejection, as I have, often seek the approval of others to try to overcome their feelings of rejection and low self-esteem. They suffer from those feelings and use the addiction to approval to try to remove the pain. They are miserable if anyone seems not to approve of them in any way or for any reason and they are anxious about the disapproval until they feel they are once again accepted. They may do almost anything to gain the approval they feel they have lost—even things their conscience tells them are wrong. For example, if a person is met with disapproval when she declines an invitation, she might change her plans and accept the invitation just to gain approval. She compromises herself for the sake of feeling approved.

An addiction is something that controls people—something they feel they cannot do without or something they do to alleviate pain or pressure. It is what people run to when they are hurting or feel lonely. It comes in many varieties, such as drugs, alcohol, gambling, sex, shopping, eating, work—and yes, even approval. Like any addict, insecure people look for a "fix" when they get shaky. They need someone to reaffirm them and assure them everything is all right and they are acceptable. When a person has an addiction the things they are addicted to are on their mind most of the time. Therefore, if a person is an approval addict, he or she will have an abnormal concern and an abundance of thoughts about what people think of them.

The good news is that none of us has to suffer with insecurity; there is a cure for the approval addiction. The Word of God says we can be secure through Jesus Christ (See Ephesians 3:17). That means we are free to be ourselves and become all we can be in Him.

THE FOUNDATION FOR SECURITY

A sense of security is something everyone needs and desires. Security enables us to enjoy healthy thinking and living. It means we feel safe, accepted, and approved of. When we are secure we approve of ourselves, we have confidence, we accept and love ourselves in a balanced way. We don't necessarily need approval from others to feel confident. Security enables us to reach our potential and fulfill our God-given destiny.

I believe it is God's will for each one of us to be secure, because lack of self-confidence torments us and keeps us from the blessings He intends for us to enjoy. Over the years I have learned that the foundation for security is knowing who we are in Christ, accepting God's unconditional love, and accepting ourselves even though we realize we have weaknesses and are not perfect.

I come from an abusive background that left me suffering from insecurities even after I became a Christian because I wasn't seeing myself through the eyes of Scripture. I rejected myself, and I didn't like myself because I didn't see myself as God saw me. I didn't know who I was in Christ (See 2 Corinthians 5:21); I wasn't rooted and grounded in His love and I didn't know I could find my approval in Him. Even though according to Scripture I had been recreated in Christ (See Ephesians 2:10) and had been made a new creature and given a fresh start and a great future, I still saw myself as a failure and someone unlovable and unacceptable.

My life was very hard during that time. I was continually frustrated and had no real peace or joy because I had a poor self-image and felt nobody liked me. Those feelings caused me to act as though I didn't need anyone—as if I didn't care how they felt about me. Yet down deep inside, I really did care and tried very hard to be what I thought others expected of me.

But as I studied the Word of God, I learned I was valuable in who I am in Christ, not in what I do or in other people's opinions of me. I realized I didn't have to stay insecure because when God looked at me, He saw the righteousness of His Son Jesus (See 2 Corinthians 5:21), not everything that was wrong with me or that I had done wrong. And the truth set me free. For the first time in my life I felt secure.

Part of our inheritance as believers is to be secure (See Isaiah 54:17)—to know who we are in Christ, to have a feeling of righteousness or rightness with God. God declares we have worth and value by the fact that He sent His Son Jesus to die for us. We are not supposed to go around all the time feeling wrong about ourselves, as so many people do. Usually people who feel that way think, *There's something wrong with me. I'm not what I need to be. I'm not where I need to be. I don't look the way I should look. I'm not talented. I don't this. I don't that. I don't something else.*

The devil likes to remind us of what we are not, but God delights in affirming us and reminding us of who we are and what we can do through Jesus. Philippians 3:3 tells us to "put no confidence or dependence [on what we are] in the flesh and on . . . external appearances," but to "glory and pride ourselves in Jesus Christ." We are to look at Jesus, not ourselves.

Insecurity stems from looking at our weaknesses, our flaws, and inabilities. Freedom from insecurity comes when we do what Hebrews 12:2 instructs us to do: look away from all that distracts us to Jesus, Who is the Author and Finisher of our faith. Our flaws will certainly distract us if we pay too much attention to them. We should confess our faults to God and trust Him to change us in His own way and timing.

KNOWLEDGE LEADS TO DELIVERANCE

Do you live under a burden of guilt and condemnation, feeling unrighteous, unworthy, and insecure? Are you a people-pleaser, always looking for the approval of others?

If the answer is yes, then I hope by the grace and the mercy of God to help you get over those feelings because they affect not only your personal relationships, but also your prayer life and your ability to be promoted in life. They certainly steal your joy and your peace—and that is not God's will for you or anyone else.

God's will is that you enjoy your life—and you can do that, if you know how. That "how" is what I want to share with you in

Approval Addiction. In the following pages are some tremendous insights I learned from God that helped me overcome the insecurities in my life and live in the righteousness, peace, and joy that are ours as children of God (See Romans 14:17). I have divided this book into three sections. Part I deals with accepting who we are in Christ—understanding we aren't perfect and that it is okay. Part II addresses some specific addictions that hinder our walk with God and with others and what we need to do to overcome them. Finally, in Part III I talk about some general truths regarding our wholeness in God and where we need to be headed in our lives if we're truly going to beat our addiction to approval. Throughout this book I will walk you through the steps and show you relevant Scriptures and personal stories that help you see you're not alone, and that there *is* ultimate triumph.

I pray that as you read this book, you will begin to experience healing and freedom. The pathway to freedom is not necessarily an easy one. But pressing forward toward that goal is definitely easier than remaining in bondage. Knowledge of your right standing with God and the truth about your righteousness leads to deliverance from such feelings as condemnation, defeat, inadequacy, insecurity, and the need for approval from people. You will be lifted to new levels of freedom and become a confident, mature person—one who can walk in the security of who you are in Christ. His approval will be all you need.

So take that first step now to overcome the Approval Addiction by taking an honest look at who you are and how you feel about yourself.

PART

I

Accepting
Who We Are

Facing Fear and Finding Freedom

The first step in understanding an out-of-balance need for approval is to understand fear. The variety of fears people deal with is endless, but an important one I discovered in my own life—and one you may be dealing with yourself—is the fear of not being pleasing to God. If you have been hurt and wounded by people who were difficult or even impossible to please, you may think God is the same way. He isn't! It is not as difficult to please God as we may think it is. Simple, childlike faith pleases Him. He already knows we will not behave perfectly all the time. That is why He sent Jesus to pay for our failures and mistakes.

As I said in the Introduction, I struggled and suffered in frustration many years trying to please God with good, or even perfect, behavior. At the same time I was always fearful I was failing. It seemed no matter what I did right, I always saw something I was doing wrong. I never felt good enough; no matter what I did, I always felt as if I needed to do more. I felt God was displeased with me, and even though that was not accurate, it was true for me because I believed it. I was deceived!

There is a possibility you, too, have been deceived. To be deceived means to believe a lie. Many people are trapped in bondage that makes them miserable simply because they have wrong belief systems. It is very possible you believe some things with all your heart, yet those things are not true at all. I once believed my future would always be affected by my past, but then I learned through God's Word that what I believed was not true at all.

We can let go of what lies behind, be totally forgiven for all our wrongdoing, and enjoy the awesome future God had planned for us since before the beginning of time.

"WHAT MUST I DO TO PLEASE GOD?"

There are two main things I believe we must do to please God. Number one is to have faith in Jesus, and number two is to desire to please Him with all our hearts. It is important to understand that we cannot have one without the other. The Bible says without faith it is impossible to please God (See Hebrews 11:6).

In John 6:28-29 we read about some people who asked Jesus:

> What are we to do, that we may [habitually] be working the works of God? [What are we to do to carry out what God requires?]
>
> Jesus replied, This is the work (service) that God asks of you; that you believe in the One Whom He has sent.

So you see God is pleased when we believe in His Son Jesus, and He is not pleased when we don't. We might do numerous good and benevolent works, yet if we have no faith in Jesus, God is still not pleased with us. But if we believe and trust in God, we enter

His rest according to Hebrews 4; we feel at ease and comfortable rather than fearful and anxious about life.

We believe, and God works. Our work—the work of the believer—is simply to believe. Remember, we are accepted because of our *faith*, not our good works. Christians are referred to as *believers*. If our job were to achieve, we would be called *achievers*, not *believers*. We often want to place an emphasis on what *we* do, but our focus should be on what God has done for us in Jesus Christ.

> *If our job were to achieve, we would be called* achievers, *not* believers.

We can concentrate on our sin and be miserable, or we can concentrate on God's forgiveness and mercy and be happy.

Once we see this truth, we can enjoy our relationship with God. We don't have to live under the pressure of acceptance by performance, followed by a fear of failure each time our performance is less than perfect. We do not have to be addicted to approval and ready to obtain it by any means. If we want to please God with all our hearts, all we need to do is believe in His Son Jesus Christ and believe what He says in His Word.

I lived in the performance-acceptance trap for many years. I was addicted to approval. I felt if I performed well, then I would be approved of and accepted by God and people. I did not feel good about nor accept myself unless I performed well. When I did not perform well, I automatically assumed God rejected me because that was what I was accustomed to with people. Once again truth was distorted for me through a wrong belief system.

God does not reject us when we make mistakes, but if we *think* He does, if we *fear* He does, the lie we have believed becomes truth to us. I once had an employee who had experienced a lot of rejection from her father when she did not do well in school or perform perfectly in other areas. The rejection she experienced early in her life caused her to develop some behavior patterns that were difficult to understand. When her job performance was anything less than perfect, I sensed her withdrawing from me and felt rejected by her. Not only did she withdraw, she also went into a work frenzy trying to get more done.

This behavior really bothered me and made it difficult for me to have a comfortable relationship with her. As her employer I dreaded giving her direction or correction about anything because I knew from experience how she would behave. As a matter of fact, I dreaded even asking her how various projects were coming along because if she could not give me a perfect report she became upset even if I remained calm. If I asked the status of her work, the only time she seemed settled and happy was if she could tell me everything was done, and done perfectly right.

I did not understand her actions at the time, but through prayer and sharing openly we finally discovered she was extremely afraid of being rejected if she did not perform perfectly. Even though I was not rejecting her, her fear of being rejected caused her to withdraw from me. To make matters worse, her withdrawal and silence made me feel *she* was rejecting *me*, or that I had done something wrong. Her belief system was wrong, and it created an uncomfortable atmosphere in which Satan could easily work.

I did not expect her to be perfect, but she expected it of herself. I was not pressuring her; she was pressuring herself. Even though I was not upset with her progress, she assumed I was and reacted to me accordingly. Her behavior really confused me and made me not want to work with her. Thankfully, she eventually learned to believe I loved and accepted her even though her performance was not always perfect. This enabled us to work together in joy for many years.

Just as I had learned before in my own life, my employee had to learn to believe what I said rather than what she felt. We must choose to do the same thing in our relationship with God. We must learn to trust God's Word more than our own feelings. We often bow down to our feelings without realizing how fickle and changeable they are. Our feelings are not a reliable source of information. God loves us and accepts us unconditionally. His love is not based on our performance. The Bible says in Ephesians 1:6 KJV that we are made acceptable in the Beloved. As I said earlier, it is our *faith* in Jesus that makes us acceptable to God and pleases Him, not our performance.

> *We must learn to trust God's Word more than our own feelings.*

We are not living by faith if we believe how we feel more than we believe what God's Word says. Do you believe the God of the Bible or the god of your feelings?

DESIRING TO PLEASE HIM IN ALL THINGS

Anyone who loves God wants to please Him. The fact that we have a desire to please Him pleases Him. To please someone means to be well thought of or approved by that person. We want God's approval, and there is nothing wrong with that. As a matter of fact, a desire to please God is necessary; it motivates us to seek His will in all things. People who have a deep desire to please God may not perform perfectly all the time, but they keep pressing forward and always have the attitude of wanting to improve.

In 2 Chronicles 16:9 we see God is searching to and fro for someone in whom He can show Himself strong, someone whose heart is perfect toward Him. The Scripture does not say He is looking for someone with a perfect performance, but rather someone with a perfect heart—a heart that desires to please Him, a heart that is grieved over sin and evil, a heart that believes in Him and His willingness and ability to forgive and restore. God knows we cannot manifest perfection. If we could be perfect in our performance, we would not need a Savior, and Jesus would have come in vain. Jesus came for those who were sick in spirit, body, and soul, not those who had no need (See Luke 5:31–32). It is acceptable to be needy!

God is a God of hearts. He sees and cares about our attitude of heart even more than our performance. I have said many times that I believe God would rather have a believer who has a good heart and a less than perfect performance than one who has a perfect performance but an impure heart.

For example, Jesus had much to say to the Pharisees of His day. They had a polished performance, they kept the laws, they followed all the rules and regulations, and they were proud of it. They also had a judgmental attitude toward others, they did not walk in love, and they showed no mercy. Jesus called them whitewashed tombs full of dead men's bones:

> Woe to you, scribes and Pharisees, pretenders (hypocrites)! For you are like tombs that have been whitewashed, which look beautiful on the outside but inside are full of dead men's bones and everything impure. (Matthew 23:27)

These Pharisees were very religious people—they kept all the rules—but their hearts were not right.

Truth pleases God. According to John 4:23–24 He is seeking worshippers who will worship Him in spirit and in truth (reality). He hates pretense! This is why I said earlier that two of the most important things to God are faith in Jesus and a pure heart that desires to please Him in all things.

A man once said to me, "I'm not mean; I'm just stupid." His description of himself was correct. He is a person whom everyone likes, and he wants to do right, yet he seems to consistently make wrong decisions that get him into trouble. It is difficult to remain angry with him because he really does not intend to cause trouble even though he frequently does.

I am sure you have met people like the man I am describing—people who are very frustrating, yet you really like them. I think God must see us that way at times. We do things that cause trouble in our own lives and then run to God to help us. The good news is that He does help us again and again because He knows our frame and remembers that we are but dust (See Psalm 103:14). As human beings, we look at the performance of others, but God sees the heart:

> But the Lord said to Samuel, Look not on his appearance or at the height of his stature, for I have rejected him. For the Lord sees not as man sees; for man looks on the outward appearance, but the Lord looks on the heart. (1 Samuel 16:7)

"THE THING I FEAR COMES UPON ME"

> For the thing which I greatly fear comes upon me, and that of which I am afraid befalls me. (Job 3:25)

As I said earlier, fear is a terrible emotion—a self-fulfilling one. Job had fears concerning his children and finally reached a place in his life where he saw his fears coming to pass. The Bible says it will be unto us as we believe (See Matthew 9:29). That principle works in the negative as well as the positive. We can receive by fear as well as by faith.

My husband and I once hired a handyman to do some work for us. He kept saying he was *afraid* he would set off the security alarm. We went over the instructions with him several times but could tell that he still lacked confidence. The first day he came to do some work, he set the alarm when he left and everything seemed to be fine. But that evening we had some bad storms, and something set the alarm off at 3:00 A.M. The police called and said a door was ajar and they had secured it. We had to call the man we hired and ask him to go check. The news that the alarm went off really unsettled him. He said, *"I was afraid that would happen."*

> *Fear is simply faith in what Satan says.*

Fear is simply faith in what Satan says. We must remember that not only does God speak to us but Satan also speaks. He is a liar (See John 8:44), and when we believe his lies, we are deceived and the door is open for him to work in our lives. We open the door for God to work by placing faith in His Word, and we open the door for Satan to work by placing faith in his word. He places thoughts in our minds that are not true, but can become true for us if they are believed. If we are afraid we are not pleasing to God or people, we will manifest behavior that will actually make us displeasing. The same principle works with rejection. If we fear being rejected, we will often behave in a way that will cause people to reject us. We produce what we believe!

Because I am seen as a strong authority figure, I sometimes encounter people who are afraid of me or very nervous in my presence. I don't do anything to make them afraid; they have a problem from something in their past that has left them insecure and fearful in the presence of authority. I don't like it when people are afraid of me. Just as in the case of my employee whose past issues strained our work relationship, it makes me uncomfortable and can actually cause me not to want to be around them. Their fear of me produces the very thing they are afraid of.

I know what I'm talking about, because I dealt with the same issue from the other side. I was raised in a very dysfunctional home—a home filled with violence, abuse, and fear. Because I was mistreated, I developed the feeling that I was flawed and unacceptable. I was ashamed of myself. I was afraid to meet new people because I felt they would not like me, and sure enough most of them did not. Even the ones I did become friends with often told me later they did not like me when they first met me. I got exactly what I believed!

GOD LOVES US!

As children of God we can renew our minds through studying God's Word and begin to think differently (See Romans 12:2). As we think differently, we will behave differently, because where the mind goes the man follows (See Proverbs 23:7). When I saw in the Word of God that He actually was pleased with me and accepted me even though I did not behave perfectly, it changed my thinking. I started *expecting* people to like me. And sure enough, they did. I even began to confess out loud that God gave me favor and that people liked me. I learned to say what God said about me instead of what the devil wanted me to believe.[1]

Ask yourself what you have been expecting out of life, and you may discover the reason behind some of your disappointments. God wants us to aggressively expect good things, not bad ones. He wants us to expect acceptance as His gift to us. God will give us favor and approval if we expect it. Satan will give us rejection and disapproval if we expect it. Living in God's supernatural favor is certainly better than attempting to earn acceptance through people-pleasing and a perfect performance.

In Matthew 3:13–17 we read an account of Jesus' baptism. When He came up out of the water, the Holy Spirit descended from heaven like a dove and landed on Him, and a voice from heaven said, "This is My Son, My Beloved, in Whom I delight!" Then, in Matthew 17:5 on the Mount of Transfiguration, a shining cloud overshadowed Jesus and His disciples, and a voice from the cloud said, "This is My Son, My Beloved, with Whom I am [and have always been] delighted." One day as I was studying, I realized that if Jesus needed to hear and receive this encouragement twice, how much more do we need to hear that we are pleasing to God? More important, what if Jesus had rejected His Father's words? How would it have affected His life and ministry?

God tries to tell us in His Word how much He loves us, that He accepts us, and that even though He already knew every mistake we would ever make, He actually chose us for Himself:

Even as [in His love] He chose us [actually picked us out for Himself as His own] in Christ before the foundation of the world, that we should be holy (consecrated and set apart for Him) and blameless in His sight, even above reproach, before Him in love. (Ephesians 1:4)

We read it, but we have a difficult time receiving it. We let our feelings steal the blessing of God's acceptance and approval. We let people's opinions determine our worth and value rather than relying on God's Word.

I encourage you to say out loud several times a day, "God loves me unconditionally, and He is pleased with me." The mind rejects such statements; after all, how could God, Who is perfect, be pleased with us in our imperfections? The point is that God separates who we are from what we do. My children are Meyers. They don't always act right, but they never stop being Meyers; they never stop being my children. Knowing they have a right heart goes a long way with me. They make mistakes, but as long as they admit it, and their heart is right, I am always willing to work with them.

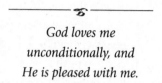

God loves me unconditionally, and He is pleased with me.

God feels the same about us. As believers in Jesus Christ, we are God's children. We may not always act the way He wants us to, but we never stop being His children.

YOU ARE NO SURPRISE TO GOD

We act as if God is shocked to discover we make mistakes. He is not in heaven wringing His hands saying, "Oh no! I had no idea you would act like this when I chose you." God has a big eraser, and He uses it to keep our record clean and clear. He knows the end from the beginning of all things (See Isaiah 46:10). He already knows what our thoughts are and every word in our mouth we haven't uttered. He is acquainted with all of our ways (See Psalm 139:1–4). Even with all His foreknowledge of our weaknesses and the mistakes we would make, He still chose us on purpose and brought us into relationship with Himself through Christ.

If we never make mistakes, then we are probably not making any decisions either. F. Scott Fitzgerald said, "Never confuse a single mistake with a final mistake." Our mistakes have value; we can learn from them. I like what author and speaker John C. Maxwell had to say about them. He said mistakes are:

M essages that give us feedback about life.

I nterruptions that should cause us to reflect and think.

S ignposts that direct us to the right path.

T ests that push us toward greater maturity.

A wakenings that keep us in the game mentally.

K eys that we can use to unlock the next door of opportunity.

E xplorations that let us journey where we've never been before.

S tatements about our development and progress.[2]

I'm reminded of an anecdote I've read and heard several times over the years. A well-known speaker started off his seminar by holding up a fifty-dollar bill. In the room of two hundred, he asked, "Who would like this fifty-dollar bill?" Hands started going up. He said, "I am going to give it to one of you, but first let me do this."

He proceeded to crumple the bill up. He then asked, "Who still wants it?"

Still the hands were up in the air.

"Well," he replied, "what if I do this?" And he dropped it on the ground and started to grind it into the floor with his shoe. He picked it up, now all crumpled and dirty.

"Now who still wants it?" Still the hands went into the air.

"My friends, you have all learned a very valuable lesson. No matter what I did to the money, you still wanted it because it did not decrease in value. It was still worth fifty dollars."

Many times in our lives, we are dropped, crumpled, and ground into the dirt by the decisions we make and the circumstances that come our way. We feel as though we are worthless. But no matter what has happened or what will happen, we will never lose our value in God's eyes. Dirty or clean, crumpled or finely creased, we are still priceless to Him.

Our desire for approval can truly be met only by receiving God's acceptance and approval of us. God told Jeremiah that before He formed him in the womb of his mother, He knew

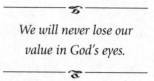

We will never lose our value in God's eyes.

him and approved of him as His chosen instrument (See Jeremiah 1:5). When God says He knows us, He means He really *knows* us. This is a knowing that leaves nothing out.

It is amazing to me that God chose me. I don't think I would have chosen me. But God's tool chest has some interesting things in it. He works with what the world would reject as useless and would throw away as trash:

> God selected (deliberately chose) what in the world is foolish to put the wise to shame, and what the world calls weak to put the strong to shame.
>
> And God also selected (deliberately chose) what in the world is lowborn and insignificant and branded and treated with contempt, even the things that are nothing, that He might depose and bring to nothing the things that are. (1 Corinthians 1:27–28)

Yes, God chooses and uses what the world would reject and throw away! Was Jeremiah perfect? Absolutely not! God had to correct him about fear, especially fear of people. Jeremiah was afraid of being rejected and meeting with disapproval. God corrected him about speaking negatively and encouraged him to go forward and not give up. God actually told Jeremiah not to look at people's faces. We pay too much attention to how people respond to us. We often watch their faces to see if they approve or disapprove of what we are wearing, our hair, our performance, et cetera.

Yes, Jeremiah had problems just like we do. When God saw Jeremiah, He did not see perfection, but He obviously did see someone with a right heart who believed in Him. He saw those two main ingredients in pleasing God: (1) faith in Jesus and (2) a deep desire to please Him. Although Jeremiah was not perfect, he did submit to the call of God on his life. Jeremiah, despite criticism, unpopularity, and attacks against him, faithfully delivered God's message to the nation of Judah.

Elijah was another great prophet. God used him mightily, and his fame was widespread, yet he also had imperfections. He experienced seasons of fear, depression, self-pity, and a desire to give up (See 1 Kings 19:3–4).

James wrote while encouraging the church to pray and believe their prayers would be answered:

> Elijah was a human being with a nature such as we have [with feelings, affections, and a constitution like ours]; and he prayed earnestly for it not to rain, and no rain fell on the earth for three years and six months. And [then] he prayed again and the heavens supplied rain and the land produced its crops [as usual]. (James 5:17–18)

James wanted to make the point that even imperfect people can pray, and God will hear. Why does God do that? Because He is pleased with faith and a heart that is right.

God is not surprised by our human behavior; actually He tries to tell us what to expect of ourselves:

> What is the nature of your life? You are [really] but a wisp of vapor (a puff of smoke, a mist) that is visible for a little while and then disappears [into thin air]. (James 4:14)

A voice says, Cry [prophesy]! And I said, What shall I cry? [The voice answered, Proclaim:] All flesh is as frail as grass, and all that makes it attractive [its kindness, its goodwill, . . . its glory and comeliness, however good] is transitory, like the flower of the field.

The grass withers, the flower fades, when the breath of the Lord blows upon it; surely [all] the people are like grass. (Isaiah 40:6-7)

The flesh (man) is like a puff of smoke or a blade of grass—here for a very short period of time and not very stable. God knows it and has no problem with it, because He is willing to work through us and show Himself strong in our weakness. Actually the Bible states that God's strength shows itself most effectively in our weaknesses (See 2 Corinthians 12:9). God has no problem with the knowledge of what we lack; we are the ones who have problems with it. We have a difficult time admitting to ourselves or anyone else that we are anything less than perfect. It is important for us to know what we can do, but even more important for us to know what we cannot do. We need to face our weaknesses, not feel bad about them.

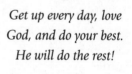

Get up every day, love God, and do your best. He will do the rest!

Get up every day, love God, and do your best. He will do the rest! Remember, God is not surprised by your inabilities, your imperfections, or your faults. He has always known everything about you that you are just now finding out, and He chose you on purpose for Himself. Jesus will present you blameless and faultless to God, if you place your trust in Him (See 1 Corinthians 1:7-8).

When we face our fears, we can find our freedom. In John 8:32 Jesus said, "The truth will set you free." The word *fear* means to run away from. We don't have to run from anything; we can confront all things in the power of the Holy Spirit. It is time to stop running, to "stand still, and see the salvation of the LORD" (Exodus 14:13).

We've talked about fear in this chapter. Now let's take a further look at what it means to be truly sure of ourselves in God, and how that helps us overcome our need for approval.

Knowing Who You Are

One of the greatest cures for approval addiction is the knowledge of who we are in Christ. According to 2 Corinthians 5:21 (KJV), we have been made the righteousness of God in Christ. The phrase "in Christ" (v. 19) is one that must be understood if we are to walk in victory. What we are in Christ is very different from what we are in ourselves. In and of ourselves we are absolutely nothing of any value, but "in Christ" we partake of everything He deserved and earned. The Bible says we are "joint-heirs" with Christ (See Romans 8:17 KJV). In Him we share His inheritance, His righteousness, and His holiness.

Learn to identify with Christ; see yourself as "in Him." The Bible teaches us in Romans chapter 6 that when He died, we died, and when He was raised to a new life, we were raised with Him. If we were to place two pennies in a jar, seal the jar, and submerge it in water, the pennies would be in the water just as much as the jar is. Actually, though, the pennies would be better off, because they would be in the same place as the jar but they wouldn't get wet.

We may use this analogy to better understand what it means to say we are "in Christ." Jesus is the jar and we are the pennies. All those who are believers in Jesus Christ are considered to be "in Him." What Jesus went through in His experience, we share. Even though we have not had the actual experience of going through it, it becomes ours through faith in Him.

Ephesians 1:17–23 and 2:5–6 teach us that we are seated with Him in heavenly places at the right hand of God. How can we be two places at once? How can we be here on earth and be seated with Him in heaven at the same time? It is possible because we live in two realms at the same time. We have a fleshly life and a spiritual one. We are spirits who have a soul and live in a body. Our feet can be touching earth, and our heart can be touching heaven.

Once we understand how God sees us through Christ, we can refrain from caring what people think about us, and feeling bad about ourselves. We don't have to be addicted to their approval, because we already have God's. We can stop living under condemnation or constantly looking for the approval of others. We can accept ourselves; and when we do so, others will begin to accept us also.

If a person is addicted to a substance, he only feels pain when he cannot get the substance. If he has a steady flow of it into his system, he will never feel pain. If we are addicted to people's approval, we will always experience pain when that approval is withdrawn—as it always is, at one time or another. However, if we look to God for our approval, we will never experience the pain of withdrawal because we have a constant, steady flow of His love and acceptance. It is always avail-

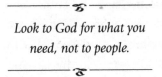

Look to God for what you need, not to people.

able for the taking. It is free and abundant. We suffer much agony because we try to get from people what only God can give us, which is a sense of worth and value. Look to God for what you need, not to people.

RIGHT WITH GOD

For our sake He made Christ [virtually] to be sin Who knew no sin, so that in and through Him we might become [endued with, viewed as being in, and examples of] the righteousness of God [what we ought to be, approved and acceptable and in right relationship with Him, by His goodness]. (2 Corinthians 5:21)

Notice that this Scripture says we are viewed by God as being righteous. That means He decides to look at us a certain way. In Ephesians 1:5 the Bible says He loved us and through Jesus Christ adopted us as His own children, and that He did it because it pleased Him and was His kind intent. In other words, God loves us because He wants to, not because of anything we do to earn or merit His love. Since He is God, He can do anything He wants to do, and He needs no one's permission to do it.

It may seem unreasonable to us that God would love us, because we look at ourselves and can find no reason for Him to do so. God does not have to be reasonable, because He is God! Just because we cannot understand what God does, does not stop Him from doing it. We understand God with our hearts, not with our heads. We may not know in our head why God loves us, but we can know in our heart that He does. People usually need a reason to love and accept us but God does not.

We need to understand that being righteous does not mean we

are so totally perfect we have no weaknesses or flaws. It means we believe Jesus became sin through His death on the cross, and by becoming sin for us, made us righteous. He actually took our sin upon Himself and paid the penalty for it. Being righteous is a state that God, by His grace, places us into through our faith in the truth of what Jesus did for us.

Righteousness—or the right way of being what God wishes or desires—is not the result of what we do, but rather what Jesus has done for us (See 2 Corinthians 5:17–21). Righteousness is imputed to us by the grace and mercy of God. God made Jesus to be sin in order to make us righteous; therefore, if we believe that truth, then we are righteous, and out of that knowledge and belief we can act right.

On the other hand, if we never believe Jesus became sin for us and made us righteous, then we will never begin to do what is right in our life. We first need to know we have been made right.

We cannot produce something we do not have. God would never expect us to produce something He did not first give us. He gives us His love and then expects us to love others. He showers us with His mercy and kindness and then expects us to be kind and merci-

We need a "righteousness consciousness," not a "sin consciousness."

ful to others. In the same way He gives us His own righteousness and expects us to behave right.

If we were apple trees, it would not be difficult for us to produce apples. We would not have to struggle to produce fruit, because it would be the natural order of things. In the same way, if we know we are right with God, the automatic response is to do right. But if we believe we are "an old, rotten sinner," then we will just keep sinning and sinning because what we do comes out of our "who"—out of who we believe we are. We need a "righteousness consciousness," not a "sin consciousness."

Under the Old Covenant people's sins could be covered by the sacrifice of the blood of bulls and goats. But the consciousness of sin could never be erased. Their sin was covered, but not removed. Under the New Covenant our sins are completely removed by the blood of Jesus, and even the consciousness of sin can be removed, because our consciences are cleansed:

> He went once for all into the [Holy of] Holies [of heaven], not by virtue of the blood of goats and calves [by which to make reconciliation between God and man], but His own blood, having found and secured a complete redemption (an everlasting release for us).
>
> For if [the mere] sprinkling of unholy and defiled persons with blood of goats and bulls and with the ashes of a burnt heifer is sufficient for the purification of the body,
>
> How much more surely shall the blood of Christ, Who by virtue of [His] eternal Spirit [His own preexistent divine personality] has offered Himself as an unblemished sacrifice to God, purify our consciences from dead works and lifeless observances to serve the [ever] living God? (Hebrews 9:12–14)

BE RELAXED IN SPIRIT

> Who is the man who reverently fears and worships the Lord? Him shall He teach in the way that he should choose.
>
> He himself shall dwell at ease. (Psalm 25:12–13)

To overcome an addiction to approval, we need to be comfortable spiritually. That statement may sound strange to you, but let me explain what I mean.

At my church in St. Louis in 1980, I had a job as the pastor's secretary. After one day I got fired. Do you know why? Because I was not a secretary; therefore I could not do what a secretary does. I could type, and I was a decent businesswoman, but that was not what God wanted me to do. It was not part of His plan for my life. I wanted that job to work out because it was my plan, but God would not allow it because He had other plans for me.

If you want to be unhappy, uncomfortable, and insecure, just spend your life trying to do something that is not right for you. It is just like trying to wear shoes that don't fit.

One time I was out shopping with a friend and I tried on a pair of shoes I really liked. They were so pretty that I wanted to buy them, but they were just a little tight.

My friend said a wise thing to me. She asked me, "Are they comfortable?"

"Oh, they're okay," I answered.

"But are they really comfortable?" she asked. "Because if they're not really comfortable, they're going to hurt your feet."

"You're right," I said. "I'm not going to buy them because I want to be really comfortable."

I thought about that incident later in my personal time with God, and I said to Him, "You know, Lord, I want to be comfortable spiritually, like being comfortable in the shoes I wear. I just want to be relaxed in spirit. I want my inner life to be at ease."

Think for a moment of any army movie you may have seen. There always comes a time when the sergeant tells all the men to stand at attention. They immediately become rigid and stiff in their stance. They don't move, and they certainly don't look relaxed. After a while the officer in charge says, "At ease," and immediately all the men relax. I believe God is speaking to His people and saying "At ease." That does not mean all of life is going to be easy, but it does mean we can do what we need to do in life with an attitude of ease.

I came to a point in my life where I wanted to be relaxed about my relationship with God and my walk with Him. I wanted to be relaxed around people and not afraid of their disapproval. I wanted to be relaxed about my gifts and calling in life. I wanted to be relaxed about everything that concerned me. I wanted to enjoy God and not spend most of my time with Him afraid He was angry because of my flaws.

I didn't want to be tied up in knots anymore. I didn't want to be tormented by fears and insecurities. I didn't want to have an ungodly need for approval—one that was so severe I would do almost anything just to feel people approved of me. I didn't want to feel condemned because of my imperfections.

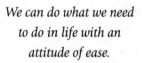

We can do what we need to do in life with an attitude of ease.

I wanted to like myself and believe I had worth and value. I wanted to know who I was in Christ and Who He could be through me if I would let Him. I wanted the reality of righteousness, peace, and joy that the Bible said I could have (See Romans 14:17).

How about you? Have you had enough tension, discomfort, and insecurity in your life? Are you tired of being tied up in knots? Tired of being afraid of what people think of you and what they may be saying about you? Do you want to be "at ease"? Well, you can relax, knowing God loves you. He accepts you in Christ, and He approves of you as His beloved child.

FIND SIMPLICITY IN CHRIST

But I fear, lest somehow, as the serpent deceived Eve by his crafti-
ness, so your minds may be corrupted from the simplicity that is in
Christ. (2 Corinthians 11:3 NKJV)

Believing God really is simple, yet we make it very complicated.
The Bible says we must become as little children or we will not
enter the kingdom of God (See Matthew 18:3). Little children are
simple. They usually believe what adults whom they trust tell
them. They don't try to figure everything out; they simply believe.
Hebrews 4 teaches us that we can enter the rest of God through
believing (See v. 3). It says we should be zealous and exert ourselves and strive diligently to enter the rest of God. We should have
knowledge of it and experience it for ourselves (See v. 11). Those
who have entered the rest of God have ceased from the weariness
and pain of human labors (See v. 10). They are not tied up in
knots; they are relaxed, secure, and free to be themselves.

We can even enter the rest of God concerning what people think
of us and whether they approve of us.
We can become so secure in Christ that
as long as we know our heart is right,
we know whatever people think of us is
between them and God and not our
concern.

> *Whatever people think of us is between them and God and not our concern.*

The apostle Paul had this kind of
confidence in Christ. In 1 Corinthians 4 we see a situation in
which Paul was being judged regarding his faithfulness. He made
it very clear he was not the least bit concerned about what people
thought of him, because he knew who he was in Christ:

But [as for me personally] it matters very little to me that I should be put on trial by you [on this point], and that you or any other human tribunal should investigate and question and cross-question me. I do not even put myself on trial and judge myself. (1 Corinthians 4:3)

GOD IS ON OUR SIDE

What then shall we say to [all] this? If God is for us, who [can be] against us? [Who can be our foe, if God is on our side?] (Romans 8:31)

According to Paul's letter to the Romans, God is for us. We also know that Satan is against us. The question we must ask is are we going to get into agreement with God or with the devil? You know the answer. Stop being against yourself just because Satan is against you!

Sad to say, sometimes we discover people are also against us. Satan works through people as well as independently. He attacks our confidence through the things people say or don't say. How important are people's opinions of us? Are we thinking for ourselves, or are we always taking everyone else's opinion? If people's opinions, judgments, and attitudes toward us are sometimes inspired by the devil, instead of agreeing with what they think and say, we must resist it.

If we know God is for us, then it shouldn't matter how we feel, or what other people think of us. As the Bible says, if God is for us, then who can be against us? If He is on our side, then what can others do to us:

So we take comfort and are encouraged and confidently and boldly say, The Lord is my Helper; I will not be seized with alarm [I will not fear or dread or be terrified]. What can man do to me? (Hebrews 13:6)

Most of us, to some extent, need to be delivered from the fear of man. We need to be completely delivered from caring what people think. People who always need the approval of others desperately want everybody to look at them from head to toe and say, "Perfect." When they do any kind of a job, they want everybody to look at it and say, "Perfect." In everything they do—the way they look, the things they say, every action they take—they want people to say, "Perfect."

If we are trying to be perfect, we are going to be disappointed—it won't work, because you and I are imperfect human beings. Even if we could manifest perfection, some people still would not be satisfied simply because they are unhappy individuals who will never be content with anything until they change their own attitudes. We need to give God our reputation and let Him be in charge of it from now on.

DON'T FEAR BEING NEEDY

I don't know about you, but I am a very needy person. Every day I tell the Lord, "Father, You are looking at a desperate woman. I need You, Lord. Without You I can do nothing."

In 1 John 1:9 the Bible teaches us that if we admit our sins and confess them, He will forgive us and cleanse us from all unrighteousness. Start by freely admitting all your faults. Hold nothing back. Admit them to God and to people. Don't make excuses or place blame elsewhere. As you do this, you will experience a new freedom, and your relationship with Jesus and with people will improve greatly. I have found that if I tell people my faults before they find them on their own, neither one of us is as bothered by them. Be open with people. Most people respect and admire honesty and openness. It is what we try to hide that comes back to haunt us.

Invite Jesus into every area of your life. Don't feel you must hide your faults from Him. He knows all about them anyway. Actually, the Lord knows more about us than we can remember or will ever discover and He loves us anyway. Give God not only what you are but especially give Him what you are not. It is easy to offer Him our strengths, but we should also offer Him our weaknesses because His strength, is made perfect in our weaknesses.

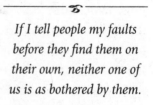

If I tell people my faults before they find them on their own, neither one of us is as bothered by them.

Don't hold anything back; give God everything! The Lord doesn't see only what we are right now, He sees what we can become if He is patient with us. He knows the plans He has for us, and they are plans for progress and success, not defeat and failure (See Jeremiah 29:11).

A thorough and complete confession of our sins gives us a good, clean, fresh feeling. It might be compared to a closet that has been closed up for a long time and is full of junk and dirt. Once it has been cleaned completely, the junk thrown away, the dirt removed, and fresh air introduced, it becomes a pleasant place. We can enjoy ourselves and feel fresh and clean once we have completely confessed our sins and received God's forgiveness of them.

A NEW AND LIVING WAY

Therefore, brethren . . . we have full freedom and confidence to
enter into the [Holy of] Holies [by the power and virtue] in the
blood of Jesus,

By this fresh (new) and living way which He initiated and dedi-
cated and opened for us through the separating curtain (veil of the
Holy of Holies), that is, through His flesh. (Hebrews 10:19–20)

Believing we are made right with God through our faith in Jesus
Christ is a new and living way, one that gives us freedom, boldness, and confidence. Trying to follow the law (trying to do everything right) in order to earn acceptance ministers death (every
kind of misery) to us; but Jesus offers us His grace, which produces
life. Grace is God's power coming to us free of charge to help us do
with ease what we could never accomplish on our own. With man
many things are impossible, but with God all things are possible
(See Matthew 19:26). Grace is freeing! It puts the burden to perform on God, rather than on the believer. As believers in Jesus
Christ, our work is to believe while God works on our behalf.

I cannot make myself acceptable to all people, and neither can
you, but we can believe God will give us favor with the people He
wants us involved with. Sometimes we try to have relationships
with people God does not even want us to be associated with.
Some of the people I really worked hard to be friends with in the
past, often compromising my own conscience in order to gain
their acceptance, were the very ones who rejected me the first time
I didn't do exactly as they wanted me to. I realize now I wanted
their friendship for wrong reasons. I was insecure and wanted to
be friends with the "popular" people, thinking my association
with important people would make me important.

Knowing who we are in Christ sets us free from the need to impress others. As long as we know who we are, we don't have to be overly concerned about what others think of us. Once we know who we are and accept ourselves, we no longer have anything to prove. When we have nothing to prove we can relax and be at ease in every situation.

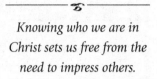

Knowing who we are in Christ sets us free from the need to impress others.

You will notice in Scripture that Jesus never tried to defend Himself, no matter what He was accused of. Why? Because He knew the truth about Himself, and that was the important thing to Him. He was not addicted to approval from people; therefore, He was free from the tyranny of what they might think of Him or say about Him. He was satisfied by the knowledge He possessed of Himself. He did not need anyone else's approval except His heavenly Father's, and He knew He had that.

True friends don't try to control you. They help you be what God wants you to be. Put your faith in God, and ask Him to give you friends who are truly right for you. Perhaps you never thought of using your faith for right friends, but God offers us a new way to live. He invites us to live by faith. There is no part of your life God is not concerned about, and He wants to be involved in everything you want, need, or do. So let Him in.

Romans 14:23 (KJV) actually states that "whatsoever is not of faith is sin." That is a strong statement, and I encourage you to meditate on it in order to gain its full meaning. *Everything* we do must be done in faith to be acceptable to God. Why? Because He knows faith is the doorway to enjoying life, and that is exactly what He wants for you and me (See John 10:10). Jesus said we can do *nothing* apart from Him (See John 15:5). We should put our faith in the Lord to help us choose right friends, as well as everything else that concerns us.

PEOPLE CAN BE SUPERNATURALLY DRAWN TO YOU

Knowing who you are in Christ will help you be confident, and as a result others will be drawn to you. People feel confident when they are with other confident people.

As an employer, I have noticed that when I ask people to do a job, and they respond with confidence, my own level of confidence in them also increases. However, if they respond insecurely or fearfully, I immediately begin to lose confidence and start wondering if they are right for the job I need done. I am strengthened by the confidence of others and weakened by their lack of confidence. We affect one another.

People look for things in other people that will make them feel better, safe, and secure. If I stepped into the pulpit to teach God's Word and appeared to lack confidence, immediately the people in my audience would lose confidence in me. They might wonder if I knew what I was doing or how I could help them if I seemed insecure myself. Satan has often tried to steal my confidence while I am teaching, but God has taught me to stand firm in this area. He has shown me that if I let Satan steal my confidence, he will gain control of the conference I am leading. When there is a disturbance in the meeting, I always strive to remain calm and confident. I know the people will follow my response. Once a water pipe burst during a conference, and water began to spray all over the people in a certain section of the building. I could see the disturbance immediately frightened everyone, because they did not understand what was going on. I remained calm and confident while I gathered information about what was happening. I assured the people they would be safe. My confidence kept them confident. If I had become frantic and fearful, there could have been a mass exodus from the building, and people might have even been hurt.

We can lead people in fear or we can lead them in confidence. We are to be confident but we are not to place our confidence in anything other than Christ Himself. Knowing our position in Him gives us confidence, and as a result people will desire friendship with us. Confident people never lack for friends. Why? Because they have what everyone wants. They have assurance and confidence, they have worth and value, and they are secure.

Confident people never lack for friends.

In this chapter we have discussed being confident in who we are and in how God sees us. In the next chapter, I would like you to take a deeper look at how important it is to understand our righteousness in God—only in believing in and living that righteousness can we begin to enjoy freedom from the misery of an addiction to approval.

CHAPTER

Conforming to Righteousness

When we accept by faith the truth that we are the righteousness of God (See 2 Corinthians 5:21) and receive it personally, we begin to conform to what we believe we are. The burden of insecurity is lifted from us; we are no longer ruled by what other people say or think about us. But a lack of understanding about righteousness can result in an approval addiction and other bondages that leave us miserable and without freedom.

The Amplified Bible describes righteousness as being made right with God and then consistently conforming to His will in thought, word, and deed (See Romans 10:3). In other words, when we are made right with God, we begin to think right, we begin to talk right, and we begin to act right. It is a *process* in which we are continually making progress. The Holy Spirit works in us, helping us become the fullness of what the Father wants us to be in Christ. The outworking of righteousness—which is ultimately seen in right thoughts, words, and actions—cannot begin until we *accept* our right standing with God through Jesus Christ. The starting point is the moment when we *believe* we are the righteousness of God in Christ according to 2 Corinthians 5:21. Once again I encourage you to say out loud what God says about you in His holy word. Say daily, "I am the righteousness of God in Christ, and therefore I can produce right behavior."

Let's take a look at what it means to think, talk, and act right with God.

THINK RIGHT

Ask yourself what you believe about yourself. Do you believe you must have approval from people in order to be happy? If so, you will never be happy when anyone disapproves of you. Do you believe you are all wrong? If you do, you will continue to produce wrong behavior. The fruit of your life will be what you believe you are. God wants us to behave right, so He gives us what we need in order to do it. God will never require us to do something without giving us what we need to do it. God gives us the gift of righteousness so we can become righteous in what we think, say, and do! Although we have sinned, God's free gift of righteousness cannot even be compared to our sin. Our sin is great, but His free gift of righteousness is greater. Our sin is swallowed up in His righteousness. Our righteousness is not found in what people think of us, it is found in Christ. He is our righteousness from God.

> For if because of one man's trespass (lapse, offense) death reigned through that one, much more surely will those who receive [God's] overflowing grace (unmerited favor) and the *free gift of righteousness* [putting them into right standing with Himself] reign as kings in life through the one Man Jesus Christ (the Messiah, the Anointed One). (Romans 5:17)

We must learn to think about and believe in our righteousness.

TALK RIGHT

> Words are powerful; take them seriously. Words can be your salva-
> tion. Words can also be your damnation. (Matthew 12:37 MESSAGE)

One of the ways we learn to talk right is by being careful what we
say about ourselves.

For several years I have known a young lady whom I'll call
Susan. Susan loves the Lord, but she comes from an abusive background. She is very insecure and a real people-pleaser. I would definitely say she is an approval addict. Susan lets people rule her
much of the time. Her decisions are influenced by what other people want
her to do rather than by what the Holy Spirit wants her to do. She says what
she thinks people want to hear. She does not follow her own heart. Susan
goes to church, but she doesn't really hear much teaching on the
biblical principles I am discussing in this chapter. She hears a lot
of teaching about laws, rules, and regulations and church doctrines, but not nearly enough about how to live her life in victory.
So she doesn't understand the importance of words, especially her
own words. She does not realize she is being defeated in life by her
own words.

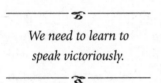

We need to learn to speak victoriously.

So many of us do the same thing. We need to learn to speak victoriously. We need to learn by faith to say about ourselves what
God says about us in His Word.

ACT RIGHT

There are many churches that teach doctrine, and that is good. We
all need a strong foundation of good solid doctrine. But along

with that doctrine, we also need to know how to live our lives. If we are going to represent Jesus properly, we need to walk victoriously. The Bible states we are more than conquerors (See Romans 8:37) and we are to reign as kings in life through Jesus Christ (See Romans 5:17). If we are defeated and lack victory, no one will want what we have. But when we are victorious, others see it and want the same victories in their lives. To put it plainly, if we want other

———— ᔓ ————

God has given us the power to make right choices and manifest right behavior.

———— ᔓ ————

people to accept Jesus, we must show them that having a relationship with Him makes a real difference in our lives. When we call ourselves Christians and go to church but repeatedly behave badly, people think we are hypocrites and phonies. God has given us the power to make right choices and manifest right behavior. How we act is important!

The realization that I was a Christian with very little victory is what urged me to seek a deeper relationship with God. That took place in 1976. As a Christian I knew I was saved by grace and that I would go to heaven when I died, but I was not enjoying the journey. I was miserable, and I had a negative attitude and life. Whatever effect I was having on others was probably not a positive one. I needed a big change. I was going to church but I did not truly know God's Word. I trusted Him for going to heaven but not for everything that concerned me. I called on Him in emergencies but did not let Him into my everyday life. God had a much better life for me than I ever dreamed, and He has the same thing for you.

Don't settle for anything less than the best God has to offer you. You can have a deep, intimate, personal relationship with God through Jesus Christ. You can enjoy daily fellowship with Him and walk in victory as you travel through this life. The Lord desires to

—————— ❧ ——————
*Don't settle for anything
less than the best God
has to offer you.*
—————— ❧ ——————

teach us how to live, how to think, how to talk, and how to act for our own good and happiness as well as to glorify Him. These principles are clearly taught in the Bible. When we diligently study the Word and allow the Lord to bless our life with truth, there is no end to what He can show us. We are His personal representatives in the earth and we need to represent Him well (See 2 Corinthians 5:20).

DOCTRINE VERSUS LIBERTY

But [as for] you, teach what is fitting and becoming to sound (wholesome) doctrine [the character and right living that identify true Christians]. (Titus 2:1)

I went to church for years and years and never heard a message about the power my words had on my life. I may have heard something about my thoughts, but if so, it wasn't enough to make any impact on my life because it did not change my thinking. I heard about grace and salvation and other good things. But it wasn't everything I needed to know in order to live in the righteousness, peace, and joy God offers to all who believe (See Romans 14:17).

There are many wonderful churches that teach God's Word in its entirety and I encourage you to make sure that wherever you choose to go to church, it is a place where you are learning and growing spiritually. We should not go to church just to fulfill an obligation we may think we have to God. We should go to church to fellowship with other believers in Jesus Christ, to worship God, and to learn how to live the life Jesus died for us to have and enjoy. We are called salt and light in the Bible (See Matthew 5:13–16). That means our lives should make people thirsty for what we have and bring a bright spot into their darkness.

Sometimes religious teaching doesn't take us far enough. It just stays in the realm of doctrine. Sometimes we get so tied up in church doctrine and rules and regulations that we never really get over into the power, victory, and freedom Jesus died to give us. For example, I was taught to pray but never told I could come "boldly" to the throne of grace. I wasn't taught about righteousness through Christ; therefore James 5:16, which states that tremendous power is made available when a righteous man prays, had no effect on my life. I tried to pray while I was filled with guilt and condemnation. I tried to pray while feeling insecure and fearful that God was not pleased with me. As a result my prayers were weak and not very effective. I learned about the principal of prayer but not the power of prayer available to the believer who understands righteousness.

Even more, I was given the impression that it was spiritual to feel unworthy and to see myself as a poor, miserable sinner. Although we have all sinned, it is not spiritual to feel bad about ourselves and be insecure—to feel as if we are no good, terrible, awful people who can never do anything right. I felt that way without Jesus, and I ended up feeling the same way after accepting Him as my Savior and Lord. That was wrong.

It is God's will—and therefore spiritual and pleasing to Him—to see ourselves in Christ. We should believe that if we have repented of our sins and accepted Jesus as our Savior, He has given us His righteousness. We are to walk in this life with our head held high because we are children of God and He loves us.

RELIGION AND RIGHTEOUSNESS

Some people within the religious community become upset with hearing someone like me talk about righteousness. I have received more judgment and criticism from some religious people over the one issue of righteousness than over anything else I teach. I have been accused of saying I am without sin, which I have never said. I know I do wrong things; I sin, but I don't concentrate on and continually fellowship with my sin. My fellowship is with the Father, the Son, and the Holy Spirit (See 1 John 1:3 KJV). Since God has made provision for our sins, I ask Him to forgive all my sins. I receive His gift of forgiveness, and then continue fellowshipping with and serving Him. I don't believe I have to add my guilt to His sacrifice. His sacrifice was complete and perfect, and no work of my flesh can improve on what He has done:

> My little children, I write you these things so that you may not violate God's law and sin. But if anyone should sin, we have an Advocate (One Who will intercede for us) with the Father—[it is] Jesus Christ [the all] righteous [upright, just, Who conforms to the Father's will in every purpose, thought and action]. (1 John 2:1)

Obviously our goal should be not to sin. But if we do sin, God has already provided Jesus, Who has been perfect in our place. He has conformed to righteousness in every area. Succumbing to a lifetime of guilt is just another form of approval addiction. We feel we are earning God's forgiveness by feeling guilty. It is our fleshly way of "paying" for our mistake. The good news is that Jesus has already paid and we can look

Succumbing to a lifetime of guilt is just another form of approval addiction.

to and identify with Him when we need forgiveness. Jesus did not die for us so we could have a religion. He died for us so we could have an intimate relationship with God through Him. He died so our sins could be forgiven and we could have a right standing with God. He died so we could come boldly to the throne of grace in prayer and have our needs met.

ARE YOU FELLOWSHIPPING WITH GOD OR WITH YOUR SIN?

The devil delights in reminding us daily of all our mistakes from the past. On Monday he reminds us of Saturday and Sunday's failures; on Tuesday he reminds us of sins committed on Monday, and so on. One morning I was spending my time with the Lord, thinking about my problems and all the areas in which I had failed, when suddenly the Lord spoke to my heart: "Joyce, are you going to fellowship with Me or with your problems?" It is our fellowship with God that helps and strengthens us to overcome our problems. We are strengthened through our union with Him. If we spend our time with God fellowshipping with our mistakes from yesterday, we never receive strength to overcome them today. Meditating on all of our faults and failures weakens us, but meditating on God's grace and willingness to forgive strengthens us:

> For by the death He died, He died to sin [ending His relation to it] once for all; and the life that He lives, He is living to God *[in unbroken fellowship with Him]*.
> Even so consider yourselves also dead to sin and your relation to it broken, but alive to God *[living in unbroken fellowship with Him]* in Christ Jesus. (Romans 6:10–11, emphasis mine)

Our relationship and fellowship is to be with God, not with our sins.

How much do you fellowship with your sins, failures, mistakes, and weaknesses? Whatever time it is, it is wasted. When you sin, admit it, ask for forgiveness, and then continue your fellowship with God. The Scripture above says we are alive to God, living in *unbroken* fellowship with Him. Don't let your sins come between you and the Lord. Even when you sin, God still wants to spend time with you, hear and answer your prayers, and help you with all of your needs. He wants you to run *to* Him, not *away* from Him!

ACCIDENTAL SIN

> No one born (begotten) of God [deliberately, knowingly, and habitually] practices sin, for God's nature abides in him [His principle of life, the divine sperm, remains permanently within him]; and he cannot practice sinning because he is born (begotten) of God. (1 John 3:9)

I like to put it this way: I used to be a full-time sinner, and once in a while I accidentally slipped up and did something right. But now that I have spent many years developing a deep, personal relationship with God and His Word, I concentrate on being a full-time obedient child of God. I still make mistakes, but not nearly as many as I once did. I am not where I need to be, but *thank God* I am not where I used to be. There are times when I accidentally make mistakes, but it is not the desire of my heart to do wrong. I do not deliberately, knowingly commit sin. I do not habitually sin. So I don't allow those occasions to make me feel insecure. I don't do everything right, but I do know that the attitude of my heart is right.

I can be having an absolutely wonderful day, feeling very close to the Lord and quite spiritual. Then my husband, Dave, comes home and says he does not care for the outfit I am wearing, and I suddenly become angry and defensive, telling him everything I don't like about him as well.

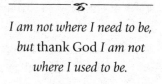

I am not where I need to be, but thank God I am not where I used to be.

I don't intend for that to happen; in fact, I plan to be very sweet and submissive when he comes home. But, as Paul said in Romans 7, the things I want to do, I don't do, and the things I don't want to do, I end up doing.

I am so glad God sees our hearts and not our sins!

I am like the man who lies in bed praying: "Dear Lord, so far today I have not done anything wrong. I have not been grouchy, selfish, or impatient. But in a few moments I am going to get up, and after that I will need a lot of help." Or, as I like to put it, I have no difficulty getting along with people when no one is at home but me!

We plan for right behavior because our hearts are right, but like Paul our plans don't always work. Thank God for His mercy that is new every day (See Lamentations 3:22–23).

COMPETITION

Just because you are a Christian does not mean you are going to do everything right all the time. But because you have been made right with God, you can stop comparing yourself to and competing with everyone else. Our acceptance is not found in being like someone else, but in being who we are through faith in Christ. Be the best "you" that you can be! Don't find some other person in the church you think is "Sister Super Christian" or "Brother Saint," someone who seems to have it all together, and then try your best to be like them. That is just the side of their nature they show at church. There may be a totally different side they show at home.

We all have our baggage we try to hide in public. Despite how wonderful we may appear to others, we all make mistakes. You are no worse than anyone else. You have strengths and weaknesses, and you do things right and you do things wrong. You sin, just as everyone else does. And sin is sin, despite its nature or magnitude. Regardless of how hard we try, none of us will ever be completely perfect in this life, but not being perfect at everything we do does not mean we have no worth or value.

You are special—unique—and that means there is only one like you, imperfections and all. My husband has a space between his front teeth. Some time ago we talked about having it fixed. After thinking about it, I told him that I would rather he leave the space there because it is part of him, and I like him the way he is. The world may consider it a flaw, but to me it is just Dave. Our children feel the same way.

> *Regardless of how hard we try, none of us will ever be completely perfect in this life.*

Competing and comparing ourselves with others can cause only two things. It can cause an attitude of pride because we deem ourselves to be better than others, or an attitude of insecurity because we deem others to be better than we are. Both of these attitudes are ungodly and should be avoided.

According to Scripture, Jesus broke down the dividing wall between people (See Ephesians 2:14). None of us has any value except what we have in Christ. Our strengths come from Him as gifts, and we cannot take credit for them. Our weaknesses are covered by His grace, and we can only thank Him for it. Since our strengths are gifts from God, it is pointless to judge our worth or value by comparing ourselves to others. If God gives the gifts, we certainly should not feel inferior just because He did not give us the same gifts He gave someone else. We all have gifts, but they differ from one another (See Romans 12:3–8).

In Scripture we see an instance in which the disciples of John the Baptist felt threatened by the popularity of Jesus' ministry. They went to John and said, "Everybody is flocking to Him." John's reply should be seriously considered by all those who feel the need to compare themselves or their gifts and abilities with others:

> John answered, A man can receive nothing [he can claim nothing, he can take unto himself nothing] except as it has been granted to him from heaven. [A man must be content to receive the gift which is given him from heaven; there is no other source.] (John 3:27)

John knew what he was sent to do, and he was doing it. He was not threatened by anyone who looked greater or better than he did. He knew that he was only responsible to be the best he could be. He was not responsible to be anyone else or even to be like anyone else.

Sometimes we seek to be like others, hoping to gain their approval. We must remember that God's approval is what we truly need, and we have it, as long as we pursue His will for our lives. God will never help us be anyone other than ourselves. I believe the Holy Spirit is grieved when we compete with others and compare ourselves with them. He wants us to be ourselves and to like who we are.

Please remember that you don't have to be like someone else to be acceptable. The world's standards are not God's. The world may say you need to be like this person or that person, but God's will is that you be yourself.

I spent many years trying to be like someone else: my husband, my neighbor, my pastor's wife, et cetera. I became so confused that I lost sight of myself. It was a great day of victory for me when I finally realized that God only wanted me to be me, that He had created me with His own hand in my mother's womb, that I was not a mistake, and that I could stand before Him as an individual without needing to compare myself with others.

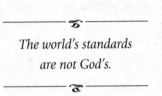

The world's standards are not God's.

Jesus is our standard, not any other person. If you are going to seek to be like anyone, let it be Jesus Himself. He is our righteousness. So embrace that righteousness, which produces feelings of being right rather than wrong, and begin to live free of insecurity.

Now let's take a look at how important having a sense of worth is to overcoming approval addiction.

Changing Your Self-Image

For as he thinks in his heart, so is he. (Proverbs 23:7)

God wants to help you change your self-image. Your self-image is the picture you carry of yourself on the inside of you. You may carry pictures of your spouse, your children, your grandchildren, or someone else in your purse or wallet. If somebody says, "Let me see a picture of your family," you open it up and show them. But what if I said to you, "Let me see the picture that you carry of yourself in your heart"? What would I see?

It is interesting to me that a lot of people don't even know they don't like themselves until I call it to their attention. I have been convinced for years that a large percentage of people's problems comes from how they feel about themselves. I think that insecurity is why some people struggle for position and power. They derive their sense of worth and value from what they do rather than from who they are. That is why some people become approval addicts, always needing the approval of others to be happy and secure. That is why some people are so competitive they can't even enjoy playing simple games. Their attitude is, "I have to win." To feel valuable, they have to be first or the best.

Many people struggle to be first. Yet Jesus said that the last will be first, and the first will be last (See Matthew 19:30). He was referring to the believing Gentiles who would be received by Him before the unbelieving Jews, but I think that Scripture can be applied to those who try to succeed without His help. Psalm 75:6,7 says that true promotion comes from God. We may manipulate circumstances and people to get a promotion, but we will never be truly happy with it. I have learned by experience that if I have to be phony and pretend and manipulate to get something, I will have to do the same thing to keep it. Eventually we become tired of living that way but find ourselves in a trap we don't know how to break free from.

THE POWER OF POSITION

Sometimes we think having a certain position will give us power, when in reality the position may end up having power over us.

I can well remember the time that I wanted a position in a church I was attending. I knew that in order to get the position I would have to be liked and accepted by a certain group of people who had the power to vote me in or out. I made all the right compliments, sent gifts, and gave invitations to dinner. I did and said all the right things again and again until I finally got what I thought I wanted. After getting the position, I soon discovered that if I did not let those people control me, they could be very vindictive. There existed a "silent" message: "We got you this position, and if you want to keep it, you had better keep us happy."

I wanted the position because at that time I needed it to feel valuable and important, yet it ended up making me feel miserable and manipulated. Whatever we gain by the works of our own flesh, we will have to maintain the same way we gained it. As soon as I did a few things these people did not like, they all rejected me. Our entire relationship was phony; they did not really like or care about me, and I really did not like or care about them.

That position was not going to make me feel permanently secure and approved of, because my real problem was "inside" me not in my circumstances. I did not need a position; I needed a revelation of God's unconditional love. I needed to seek God's approval, not man's approval.

> *Until we accept and approve of ourselves, no amount of approval from others will keep us permanently secure.*

Until we accept and approve of ourselves, no amount of approval from others will keep us permanently secure. The outside approval we seek becomes an addiction. We work to get approval or a compliment and it feels good for a short while, and then we find that we need another and another and another. True freedom never comes until we fully realize that we don't need to struggle to get from man what God freely gives us: love, acceptance, approval, security, worth, and value.

The world is full of pretense, and sad to say the church is not immune to it. People play some of the same silly games in church that they play in the world. They vie for position and power for all the wrong reasons.

I had a poor self-image, so I tried to enhance my image through position. What I really needed was to know that I was valuable to God as a person totally apart from my position in life. I am the president of *Joyce Meyer Ministries,* which is a worldwide ministry with eight foreign offices in addition to the one in the United States. My position sounds important, but I have learned from past experience not to let my sense of worth and value become attached to what I do. Should the time ever come when I can no longer do what I am doing, I want the assurance and confidence that I am still equally as valuable to God apart from my work.

I encourage you not to let your value become attached to a position. Positions can come and go in life, but God and His love for you remains. God is not impressed with the positions that people hold (See Galatians 2:6). The bottom line is, if we know who we are in Christ, then we can have a healthy self-image apart from our position or job title.

I also held a position at a different church in St. Louis, Missouri, for many years. When God told me it was time to lay it down and start my own ministry, I had a difficult time being obedient. Actually I was not obedient for quite some time, and the longer I remained in disobedience, the more miserable I became. I liked my position. I had a title, a parking place with my name on it, a guaranteed seat on the front row of the church, and everyone's admiration. I was on the "inside." I always knew what was going on. I actually did not realize how dependent I was on the position to give me feelings of security until God told me to walk away from it.

I finally did obey God, but I was shaken to the core by the feelings I experienced after I left the position. I still attended church there, but I felt really out of place each time I went to a service. My seat and my parking place had been given away, all kinds of things were going on that I knew nothing about, and I didn't know where I belonged anymore. God had to teach me that my place is in Him, and that as long as I know that fact, I don't have to be uncomfortable anywhere with anyone.

Have you ever felt like all the props in life have been kicked out from under you? If so, consider that God may be doing you a huge favor. Sometimes we are "propped up" by people or positions, and the only way we realize it is to have those things removed. A prop is something that holds something else in place, something that makes it secure. God wants our security to be in Him, not in things. He is the only thing in life that is not shaky, the only thing that is certain and sure. God allows some "props" in life while we are getting rooted in Him, but eventually He removes all those other

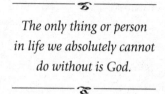

The only thing or person in life we absolutely cannot do without is God.

things we have depended on excessively. It frightens us initially, but it ends up being the best thing that ever happened to us. When we don't have anyone else, we develop a deep relationship with God that will carry us through anything life brings our way.

If you feel right now that you have lost something or someone that you just cannot do without, you are wrong. The only thing or person in life we absolutely cannot do without is God. He is our Strength, our Stronghold in times of trouble, our High Tower, our Hiding Place, and our Refuge (See Psalm 9:9; 31:4; 32:7; 37:39; 46:11).

When I lost my friends, and again when I lost my position at church, I hurt so much emotionally I thought I would not survive. These events eventually helped me realize that I depended entirely too much on people and their opinion of me. I depended on my position. I thought if I held a high position then people would think well of me and accept me. God removed it all and taught me the things I hope to teach you in this book. Our worth and value, our acceptance and approval, come from Him. As long as we have that, we have the most valuable thing in the world.

When we need what the world offers in order to feel good about ourselves, God often withholds it. Once we no longer *need* those things, He can give them to us, because they will not control us. Now I have friends, influence, position, authority, acceptance, et cetera, but the key to keeping them is knowing beyond a shadow of doubt that I don't have to have them to be happy and fulfilled.

I am convinced that as long as we keep God first in our life, He will give us everything else. However, if we allow anything else to take His place, He will become jealous and remove it.

FACE THE TRUTH, AND BE FREE

And you will know the Truth, and the Truth will set you free. (John 8:32)

It is interesting to me that there is only one thing that will set us free, and that is the truth. Yet that is the one thing we have a hard time dealing with. We don't mind facing the truth about everyone else so much, but when it comes to facing the truth about ourselves, it is quite a different matter.

It was difficult for me to face the fact that my security was tied up in the position I held. It was hard for me to say at that time, "I am insecure, I don't like myself, and I need God's help and healing in this area of my life." But as I always say, there are two kinds of pain in the world: the pain of never changing, and the pain of changing. If I had refused to face the truth, I would still be in bondage. I would still be trying to please people, addicted to approval in order to keep a position that I probably would not even like. As it is, I am free. I know who I am in Christ apart from what I do. I want to please people, but I am not devastated if they are not pleased with me. As long as I know my heart is right, that is sufficient. If I am doing the best I can and people don't approve, what they think will have to be between them and God.

I want approval—nobody wants to be disapproved of—but I am not addicted to it. I enjoy it, but if I have to live without it, I can. I went through the pain of facing truth and change, and it brought me freedom. The only way out of bondage is to go through what we need to go through.

I strongly encourage you to be careful not to let anything become more important to you than it should be. Keep God first so He can bless you with other things you desire. As Matthew 6:33 (NKJV) says, "Seek first the kingdom of God and His righteousness, and all these things shall be added unto you."

FAILING DOES NOT MAKE YOU A FAILURE

Don't see yourself as a failure just because you have failed at certain things in the past. Nobody is good at everything. Don't let the picture you carry of yourself, your self-image, be marred by past mistakes. Sometimes the only way we can find out what we are meant to be doing in life is to step out and try some things. The process of elimination is often helpful, but we may make some mistakes in the process.

> *Sometimes the only way we can find out what we are meant to be doing in life is to step out and try some things.*

When I was seeking God's will for my life in ministry, I tried working in the nursery. It didn't even take two weeks of time to know that was not my ministry. I knew it, and so did the children. I also tried street ministry, and although I did it, I was very uncomfortable and actually disliked it very much. At first I felt guilty that I didn't want to go out on the streets and tell people about Jesus, but later I realized that if God had intended that type of ministry for me, He would have given me a gift and a desire in that area. I mentioned earlier that my first church job was as secretary to my pastor, and I got fired the first day. Just because I failed at that job does not mean I am a failure; I have gone on to be quite successful.

GETTING PAST YOUR PAST

A lot of people let the past dictate their future. Don't do that! Get past your past. We all have a past, but we all have a future. The Bible teaches us in Ephesians 2:10 that we are recreated in Christ Jesus so we might do the good works He planned beforehand for us and live the good life He prearranged and made ready for us. The word *recreated* indicates we were created, messed up, and in need of repair. In Jeremiah 18:1–4 we read of the potter who had to remake his vessel because it had been marred. That is a picture of us in the hands of the Lord, the Master Potter.

We are said to be new creatures when we enter into a relationship with Christ. Old things pass away. We have an opportunity for a new beginning. We become new spiritual clay for the Holy Spirit to work with. God makes arrangements for each of us to have a fresh start, but we must be willing to let go of the past and go on. We make a way for the new by *believing* what God says about it:

> For I know the thoughts and plans that I have for you, says the Lord, thoughts and plans for welfare and peace and not for evil, to give you hope in your final outcome. (Jeremiah 29:11)

Satan wants us to have a negative attitude and to feel hopeless, but God's Word says we should be "prisoners of hope":

Return to the stronghold [of security and prosperity], you *prisoners of hope;* even today do I declare that I will restore double your former prosperity to you. (Zechariah 9:12, emphasis mine)

Don't ever stop hoping. Romans 4 teaches us that Abraham had no human reason to hope that God's promise would be fulfilled, but he hoped on in faith. It says that no doubt or unbelief made him waver concerning the promise of God, but he grew strong as he gave praise and glory to God. Abraham remained positive and hopeful, and we know from the Bible that he received his prom-

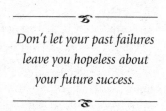

Don't let your past failures leave you hopeless about your future success.

ised blessing of a child. Don't let your past failures leave you hopeless about your future success. Your future has no room in it for the failures of the past. As I have stated, just because you have failed at some things does not make you a failure.

Whatever Satan has stolen through deception, God will restore doubled, if you are willing to press forward, forgetting the past. You have to let go in order to go on!

PEOPLE WITH A PAST

Mary Magdalene was a woman with a past. She had sold her love by the hour; she was a prostitute. She was called "an especially wicked sinner" by the Pharisees (See Luke 7:37). She was called Magdalene because she was from Magdala, which was an unremarkable town. Of Jesus' hometown of Nazareth, the people said:

"Can any good thing come out of Nazareth?" (John 1:46). I mention these two examples to show you God does not always choose people from popular places with a lot of skills and a lovely past.

In Luke 7:36–50 we see the account of Mary anointing Jesus' feet with a bottle of very expensive perfume, washing them with her tears, and drying them with her hair. Since she was a prostitute, the perfume was probably either a gift from one of her clients or was purchased with money she had earned from her profession. At one time Jesus cast seven demons out of her (See Luke 8:2). Her act of love was seen by other people as being erotic because of her past, but Jesus knew it was an act of pure love.

When we have an unpleasant past, people often misjudge our actions, and we find ourselves caught up in the approval game, trying to convince others that we are acceptable. People don't forget our past as easily as God does. The Pharisees could not understand Jesus' allowing Mary to even touch Him. Jesus said that those who have been forgiven much will love much (See Luke 7:47). Mary knew her past well; she loved Jesus greatly because He had forgiven her for her great sins. She wanted to give Him the most expensive thing she owned; she wanted to serve Him. He saw her heart, not her past.

Mary showed humility by the fact that she was at Jesus' feet. Some want to be at His head, but not many are seeking to kneel at His feet. Many want to know what He knows, to be in on the planning, and to sit in positions of leadership. Our position does not impress God, but our posture does. Where are you postured?

Mary traveled with Jesus in His ministry and supported Him out of her property and personal belongings (See Luke 8:2–3). It is possible that her wealth came from her past. You may have useable things from your past—some experience, some wisdom gained, or even some material goods—that can now be used in the kingdom.

Mary was at the crucifixion of Jesus (See John 19:25). She did not disappear when the going got rough. She stayed with Him until the end. Mary was at the tomb and found it empty (See John 20:1–13). The first words spoken at the empty tomb were to a woman. The angel said, "Go quickly and tell His disciples, He has risen from the dead" (Matthew 28:7). Jesus met Mary as she went, and when she recognized Him she clasped His feet and worshipped Him. He told her, "Go and tell My brethren to go into Galilee, and there they will see Me" (vv. 9–10).

My main points are these: Mary was a woman with a past, Jesus forgave her, and she certainly had a great future. She has been talked about in every generation since Christ, and the stories from her life give us many rich examples that can be applied to our own lives. She could have succumbed to approval addiction and spent her life being miserable, but she put her trust in Jesus and embraced her new life in Him.

Will God use us if we have a past? I am not sure He can use us if we don't have some kind of past. We gain experience by the things we go through. Much of my teaching comes from my past. I have a past, I have applied the Word of God to it, and I am enjoying the future God promised me.

Let's look at a few more people who had questionable pasts—and that God still used mightily.

PETER

Peter was a man with a past. He was no one special; he was just a fisherman, and a rather rough, crude one at that. Peter was bold and not afraid of change, but he also had many faults. In Matthew 16:22–23 we see Peter trying to correct Jesus. In Matthew 26:31–35 we see that Peter thought more highly of himself than he should have. He had a pride problem and saw himself as better than other men. In Matthew 26:69–75 it is recorded that Peter denied even knowing Jesus.

Once Peter realized the depth of his sin, he wept bitterly, which showed that he had a repentant heart (v. 75). God is merciful and understands our weaknesses. In Mark 16:1–7 we learn that when Jesus sent a message to His disciples that He was risen from the dead, His messenger, the angel, especially mentioned Peter by name saying, "Tell the disciples and Peter, He goes before you into Galilee" (v. 7). I can just imagine the joy Peter felt when he was told that Jesus had sent him a personal message. Peter had been included in God's plans for the future even though he had a past record of foolishness and failure. Peter had denied Christ, and yet he became one of the best-known apostles. Peter could have spent his entire life feeling bad about his denial of Jesus, but he pressed past that failure and became valuable to God's kingdom. He had so much Holy Ghost power that when his shadow fell on people, they were healed (See Acts 5:15)!

> *God promises to forget our past mistakes.*

God is willing to forgive those who make mistakes, but they must be willing to receive His forgiveness. They must also forgive themselves. God promises to forget our past mistakes (See Jeremiah 31:34). Stop remembering what God has forgotten!

JACOB

Jacob was a man with a past. He had been a schemer, a trickster, and a swindler. He was a liar. He was also selfish and sometimes downright cruel to others. He took advantage of people in order to get what he wanted. Jacob used his brother Esau's weak state to steal his birthright. He lied to his father, pretending to be Esau in order to receive the prayer of blessing that belonged to the first-born.

The Bible teaches that we reap what we sow (See Galatians 6:7), and sure enough the time came in Jacob's life when he received treatment from his uncle Laban similar to what he had given others. Laban cheated Jacob, who wanted to marry Laban's daughter Rachel, promising him he could do so if he worked seven years as payment for her. After his seven years of labor were completed, Jacob expected to receive Rachel but was given her sister Leah instead. He was then told he would have to work another seven years for Rachel. I am sure Jacob felt deceived, cheated, and unfairly treated. He probably failed to remember that he had treated people the same way on several occasions. Yes, we reap what we sow. What goes around, comes around.

Eventually, Jacob experienced a change of heart. He became tired of running and hiding from Esau. Jacob finally left everything he had and returned to his homeland. On the way, he began to wrestle with God. He was determined to receive a blessing from God no matter what it cost him. God changed Jacob's name, which meant trickster, schemer, and swindler, to Israel, which meant contender with God (See Genesis 32:27–28). Jacob went on to become a great leader and man of God. He had a past that could have easily labeled him a failure, but once he faced it and repented of it, he also had a future (Read about Jacob in Genesis 25–32).

RUTH

Ruth was a Moabitess. She worshipped idols, and yet she decided to serve the one true God and as a result ended up in the direct blood-line of David and Jesus. (See the book of Ruth and Matthew 1:5).

RAHAB

Rahab was a harlot, and yet she helped God's people and, like Ruth, ended up in the bloodline of David and Jesus (See Joshua 2 and 6 and Matthew 1:5).

PAUL

Paul had a past. He persecuted Christians and yet became the apostle who received two-thirds of the New Testament by direct revelation and was taken into the third heaven where he saw glories he could not even describe (See 2 Corinthians 12:1–4). When handkerchiefs and aprons were taken from his body and placed on the sick, the sick were healed (See Acts 19:11–12). That is a powerful anointing! It certainly does not seem that Paul's past affected his future.

MATTHEW

Matthew had a past; he was a despised tax collector who became one of the twelve disciples (See Mark 2:14).

The past you are dealing with could be the past of ten years ago or the past of yesterday, but the past is the past! Paul said in Philippians 3:10–15 that letting go of the past was one thing he worked diligently to do. Feeling condemned about the past is failing to accept God's forgiveness of it. Feeling that your past can adversely affect your future is refusing to let go of it. God is still God, and He can work good out of anything, if we give Him an opportunity to do so by believing! *All things* work out for good to those who pray, love God, and want His will in their lives (See Romans 8:28 KJV).

YOU WILL SUCCEED IF YOU REFUSE TO STOP TRYING

Did you know Abraham Lincoln—who was probably one of our greatest presidents, if not the greatest—lost several elections before he was elected president of the United States? As a matter of fact, he tried to get elected to public office so many times and failed so often that it's hard to understand how he could ever have the nerve to run for president. Yet, he did—and won.

Did you know Thomas Edison once said: "I failed my way to success"? He refused to quit trying, and he finally invented the light bulb, but he had two thousand failed experiments trying to invent it before he succeeded. A person like Edison who will not give up is an individual of strong character.

Did you know the material used to manufacture Kleenex tissues was originally invented as a gas mask filter during World War I, but it failed? Since it didn't work, the inventors tried making a facial tissue for removing cold

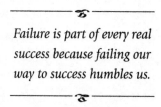

Failure is part of every real success because failing our way to success humbles us.

cream, but that approach wasn't successful. They finally hit upon a success when it was repackaged as a disposable handkerchief, and now Americans buy two hundred billion Kleenexes a year. It started out as two failures, but somebody said, "I refuse to give up!"[1]

I personally believe failure is part of every real success because failing our way to success humbles us. It is a vital part of God's being able to use us effectively.

Charles Darrow set a goal when he was in his twenties; he determined that he was going to be a millionaire. This isn't all that unusual today, but back then, it was extremely unusual. Charles lived during the Roaring Twenties, a time when a million dollars was an enormous sum. He married a woman named Esther, promising her that one day they would be millionaires. Then tragedy struck in 1929—the Great Depression. Both Charles and Esther lost their jobs. They mortgaged their house, gave up their car, and used all their life savings. Charles was absolutely crushed. He sat around the house depressed until one day he told his wife she could leave him if she wanted to. "After all," he said, "it's clear that we're never going to reach our goal." Esther wasn't about to leave. She told Charles they were going to reach their goal, but they would need to do something every day to keep the dream alive.

What she was trying to tell Charles was this: Don't let your dreams die just because you made a few mistakes in the past. Don't give up just because you tried something a few times, and it didn't seem to work. God wants you to press on past mistakes. The devil wants you to give up. Progress requires paying a price, and sometimes the price you pay for progress is just to "keep on keeping on" and saying: "I'm not going to quit until I have some kind of victory." Don't be the kind of person whose way of dealing with everything hard is: "I quit!"

Esther Darrow told her husband: "Keep your dream alive." Charles responded: "It's dead. We failed. Nothing's going to work." But she wouldn't listen to that kind of talk; she refused to believe it. She suggested that every night they take some time to discuss what they would do toward reaching their dream. They began doing this night after night, and soon Charles came up with an idea of creating play money. His idea was something quite appealing since money was so scarce in those days. Since they were both out of work, he and Esther had lots of time, and now they had lots of easy money to play with. So they pretended to buy things like houses, property, and buildings. Soon they turned the fantasy into a full-fledged game with board, dice, cards, little houses, hotels . . .

You guessed it. It was the beginning of a game you probably have in your closet right now; it's called Monopoly.

Charles's family and friends enjoyed the game, and in 1935 they persuaded him to approach a game company called Parker Brothers to see if they would buy it. The executives played the game and said: "It's dull, slow, complex, and boring; we don't want to buy it."

Well, Charles persevered. Perseverance is vital to success. We must persevere, be steadfast, keep on keeping on, and refuse to give up. When we do that, we will eventually succeed.

Charles's wife kept encouraging him. Thank God for the people in our lives who encourage us! He approached Wanamaker's toy store and told an executive that if they would stock the game, he would get a five-thousand-dollar loan and make several of the games because he believed they would sell. The game took off, and suddenly Parker Brothers became interested. The company executives now replayed the game, and this time found it imaginative, fast-paced, and surprisingly easy to master. The game was copyrighted in 1935, and Parker Brothers bought it from Charles Darrow for one million dollars. Charles and Esther's dream came true.[2]

We love to read success stories like this one, but let us remember that God wants to do the same type of thing through each of us. He is "no respecter of persons" (Acts 10:34). That means He does not have a few favorite

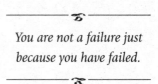

You are not a failure just because you have failed.

people, and all the rest are left out. God's principles will work for anyone who is willing to work them. His Word says all things are possible to the one who believes (See Mark 9:23). If we stay positive, keep on believing, and refuse to give up, God will do something great through all of us.

Don't get so caught up in the number of failed attempts in your life that you refuse even to believe you have a future. Remember, you are not a failure just because you have failed. God sees your worth no matter what; there's no need for any approval but His, and if He can overlook your past, so can you.

In the next chapter I am going to ask you to take a closer look at what it means not only to understand your worth, but to love and approve of yourself.

CHAPTER

5

Loving Yourself

The Bible teaches us we are to love our neighbor as we love our-selves (See Matthew 22:39). What if we don't love ourselves? It renders us incapable of loving others, which is a big problem. The distinguishing mark of Christians is their love walk:

> I give you a new commandment: that you should love one another. Just as I have loved you, so you too should love one another.
>
> By this shall all [men] know that you are My disciples, if you love one another [if you keep on showing love among yourselves]. (John 13:34–35)

People who cannot love and approve of themselves live in tremendous emotional pain. If they don't approve of themselves, they may end up with an addiction to approval from others. God has not created us for rejection, but acceptance. He accepts us by virtue of our faith in Christ, and we must receive His acceptance by accepting ourselves. People who reject and even hate themselves are doomed to a life of misery and failure.

How do you feel about yourself? Many people don't know how they feel about themselves because they have never taken time to think about it. You should. You do have a relationship with yourself. Actually, you have to be with yourself all the time. You are the one person you never get away from. If you don't like yourself, if you don't get along with yourself, you are doomed to misery.

If you don't believe that is so, all you need do is remember a time when you had to spend a day or longer with someone you absolutely did not like or perhaps even really despised. It was likely a miserable time, one that you would avoid repeating. You need to realize that not liking yourself is essentially fostering those same feelings! As a Christian, you were not made to hate yourself, but to love yourself and to enjoy the good life God has given you. Since God loved us so much that He sacrificed His only Son for us, it is rather disrespectful and insulting to Him for us to despise ourselves.

ENJOYING LIFE

Enjoying life is impossible if we don't enjoy ourselves. You might ask, "Joyce, how can I enjoy myself? I do too many dumb things and make too many mistakes to enjoy myself." Perhaps you don't like the way you look, or your personality, or even one particular feature of your body.

If that is the case, I understand how you feel. For many years I disliked my voice so much I was almost paranoid about it. I actually dreaded opening my mouth and letting someone hear me speak for the first time because I felt my voice was not one a woman should have. If you have ever heard me speak, you know my voice is very deep for a female. Quite often when I make phone calls, people who don't know me think I am a male. They call me Mr. Meyer. There were times when that made me angry, embarrassed me, and added to my feelings of insecurity.

The interesting thing is that my voice is what God is using most. He has chosen to use me in a media ministry where my voice is heard in most of the world daily. God can take what we think is a flaw and do great things with it. As a matter of fact, He delights in doing just that. As we have seen, His strength is made perfect in our weaknesses; He shows Himself strong through what we would discard as having zero value.

Make a decision today to develop a new and more positive attitude toward yourself.

What don't you like about yourself? Be specific; take an inventory and make a decision today to develop a new and more positive attitude toward yourself.

Jesus died so we could have life and enjoy it (See John 10:10). Living with daily self-rejection, or even self-hatred, is a horrible way to live. We project to others what we feel about ourselves. If we want other people to have a good opinion of us, we must begin by having a good opinion of ourselves. Most of the time people don't love and approve of themselves; therefore, they seek from others what they should be getting from God, which is a sense of being valuable and lovable. When they don't get from other people what they seek, they feel rejected, and the negative feelings they have about themselves increase. This type of negative self-attitude is an open door for Satan. According to the Bible, he looks for those whom he may devour (See 1 Peter 5:8). People who don't know how to love themselves in a balanced way are a gourmet meal for the enemy.

A BALANCED ATTITUDE

A fear of being prideful may keep a person trapped in an attitude of self-abasement. The Bible does teach us not to have an exaggerated opinion of our own importance (See Romans 12:3). We are to estimate ourselves according to the grace of God, knowing that our strengths come from Him and make us no better than others. We *all* have strengths and weaknesses! The Word of God says He gives gifts unto men, and He chooses who will receive what gifts (See 1 Corinthians 12:4–11). We cannot simply select what we want to be good at.

Knowing our gifts come from God, we are not to critically appraise or look down on someone who is unable to excel at the same things we do. We definitely need to avoid pride: "Pride goes before destruction, and a haughty spirit before a fall" (Proverbs 16:18). Pride is very dangerous. Many great men and women of God have fallen into sin due to pride.

Don't fall into the trap of pride, but don't go to the other extreme and think that self-rejection, self-hatred, and self-abasement is the answer. Instead, seek to be what I call an "everything-nothing" person—everything in Christ and nothing without Him. Jesus Himself said, "Apart from Me . . . you can do nothing" (John 15:5). Be confident, but remember the strength that comes from confidence can quickly be lost in conceit. It is vital to remain humble. I know I can do nothing of any real value unless Christ is flowing through me. He deserves all the credit and glory for any good work that manifests through us. The apostle Paul said, "I know that nothing good dwells within me" (Romans 7:18). In and of ourselves we can claim nothing good. Only God is good, and whatever good thing comes from us is merely a manifestation of

His working through us (See Matthew 19:17). Don't fail to give God the credit for your successes.

When people compliment me, as they often do, I graciously receive their kind remarks and promptly lift them up to the Lord. I tell Him that I know exactly what I am without Him and that He is truly the One Who deserves the compliment. God shows Himself strong in those who are humble enough to allow Him to do so. Although we ourselves are nothing, we are vessels for Him to flow through:

> However, we possess this precious treasure [the divine Light of the Gospel] in (frail, human) vessels of earth, that the grandeur and exceeding greatness of the power may be shown to be from God and not from ourselves. (2 Corinthians 4:7)

CRACKED POTS

God works through jars of clay, or what I often call "cracked pots." This means we are flawed, so when people look at us and see amazing things happening, they know it must be God at work because it certainly could not be us. I believe anyone who really knows me does not have any difficulty realizing the work I am doing on the earth today certainly must be God at work in and through me. They give Him the glory, not me, because they see my imperfections and know my limitations. God chooses the weak and foolish things on purpose so no mortal can have pretense for glorying in His presence (1 Corinthians 1:27–29).

Imagine a pot with a lamp in it and a lid on it. Even though it may be filled with light, no one can see the light within it. Yet if the pot is cracked, the light will shine through the cracks. In this same way, God works through our imperfections.

Can you love a cracked pot? God can! It is godly to love yourself in a balanced, healthy way. It is ungodly to reject and despise yourself.

SELF-ACCEPTANCE

The Word of God instructs us to desire peaceful relations with God, with ourselves, and with our fellow man (See 1 Peter 3:11). It actually says we are not merely to desire them, but to pursue and go after them. It stresses the importance of having good relationships in all three areas. I like to say that the Bible is a book about relationships. It has a great deal to say about our relationship with God. Everything starts with the development of our relationship with the Father through His Son Jesus Christ. We are to be at peace with God and experience His love. God's Word also talks extensively about our relationships with other people. Teachings on love, proper attitudes, serving others, and giving abound in the Bible. The Bible also teaches us about the importance of having a proper attitude toward ourselves. It teaches us about our relationship with ourselves.

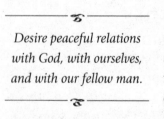

Desire peaceful relations with God, with ourselves, and with our fellow man.

Do you have a critical, faultfinding attitude toward yourself? If so, you are out of God's will. Paul refused to sit in judgment on himself, and he paid no attention to anyone else who did judge him:

> But [as for me personally] it matters very little to me that I should be put on trial by you [on this point], and that you or any other human

tribunal should investigate and question and cross-question me, I do not even put myself on trial and judge myself. (1 Corinthians 4:3)

Paul was confident in Christ. Because he knew he was made acceptable to God in Christ, he accepted himself. He also knew who he was in Christ. He knew where he came from, and he knew where he was headed. I am sure Paul remembered his past and how he had vehemently persecuted Christians prior to God's opening his eyes to the truth. He said himself that he had to make an effort to let go of the past and press on toward perfection. He also clarified that he did not think he had arrived (See Philippians 3:12–14). In other words, Paul did not claim perfection, but neither did he have a bad attitude toward himself. He knew he made mistakes, but he did not reject and despise himself because of them.

The type of confidence we see displayed by Paul is very freeing. It reminds us that Jesus died so we could be free: "So if the Son liberates you [makes you free men], then you are really and unquestionably free" (John 8:36).

God wanted so much to see His children free and able to enjoy life that He was willing to send His only Son to die in order to insure that freedom (See John 3:16). He purchased our freedom with the blood of His Son. The very least we can do is learn to see ourselves the way He sees us, which is precious and valuable. God would not let Jesus die for a bunch of junk, for people with no value and no purpose. And Jesus would not have given Himself to die on our behalf if we had been of no worth or value to God. After all, it was Jesus

Who gave Himself on our behalf that He might redeem us (purchase our freedom) from all iniquity and purify for Himself a people [to be peculiarly His own, people who are] eager and enthusiastic about [living a life that is good and filled with] beneficial deeds. (Titus 2:14)

Are you moping around, depressed, discouraged, and despondent? Do you spend so much time thinking about all of your faults that you have lost your hope and enthusiasm about living a good life? If so, please make a change today. Choose a new attitude toward yourself. Paul had to make that choice, I had to make it, and you must make it also if you want to glorify God with your life.

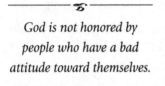

God is not honored by people who have a bad attitude toward themselves.

God is not honored by people who have a bad attitude toward themselves; in fact, as I said previously, it is downright insulting to Him. If you loved and valued a group of people so much that you were willing to suffer horribly and die for them so they could enjoy themselves and their lives, how would it make you feel if they refused your gift? I hope and pray you are beginning to see what I am trying to say.

Paul said that he pressed on to lay hold of that for which Christ Jesus had laid hold of him and made him His own (See Philippians 3:12). He was speaking of the quality of life Jesus wanted him to have. Paul knew that he did not deserve it, but for Jesus' sake he was determined to have it. Can we do any less?

SUPER SHEEP

I am the Good Shepherd. The Good Shepherd risks and lays down His [own] life for the sheep. (John 10:11)

Jesus referred to God's children as sheep, and for a good reason. Sheep are not known to be the most intelligent animals in the world. They need a shepherd. Without guidance and help, they will do things that can even be self-destructive: "All we like sheep have gone astray, we have turned every one to his own way" (Isaiah 53:6). Sheep are stubborn, which is another reason God uses the analogy to describe us. We often choose to do things that will turn out badly for us unless God intervenes. Sheep actually have many faults, but they don't try to hide them. Their simple willingness to be what they are is one of their few strengths. We try to hide our faults, and the fact that we do becomes one of our biggest problems. God knows everything anyway, so why do we try to hide anything from Him? We try to be "super sheep," and there is no such thing. The words *super* and *sheep* don't even go together.

DON'T BE AFRAID OF THE LIGHT

The light of God exposes things (See John 3:20 and 1 Corinthians 4:5). When the light is turned on in a room, we can see the dirt and the bugs that begin to scurry. God is Light (See 1 John 1:5). When He gets involved in our lives, He begins to show us things we may prefer not to look at, things we have kept hidden, even from ourselves. We are frequently deceived, especially about ourselves. We prefer not to deal with our faults, nor do we delight in having them exposed. We may feel condemned about them, but at least we feel they are hidden. Anything hidden has power over us because we fear it may be found out. The best and most freeing thing we can do is face up to what God wants to expose and get beyond the fear of it.

For many years I hid the fact that I had been sexually abused by my father. I saw it as a weakness and something to be ashamed of. I felt as if there was something wrong with me, that I was second-hand merchandise. Because I was afraid of anyone knowing about my past, it continued to have power over me. When the Holy Spirit began leading me to share the details of my abusive past, I would shake violently. I was terribly afraid of my past. What would people think? Would they reject me? Would they blame me or hate me? The devil had lied to me for at least twenty-five years about how people would view me if they knew about my past, so I worked hard at keeping it a secret.

I often told lies about my past and my parents. If someone asked me about my childhood, I avoided mentioning anything that might cause suspicion. But when it was finally brought out into the light, the exact opposite of what I thought would happen took place. People responded with compassion, not judgment. My testimony began helping others who were also locked in a prison of fear. The more I shared my past, the less power it had over me. God's light exposed Satan's lies, and the truth made me free.

Most of us want to hide anything we perceive as a weakness or imperfection, but I encourage you to expose everything to the open light of God's love. We have already seen that God chooses and uses people with flaws. Refusing to admit that we have them may disqualify us from being used by God. He wants truth, not deception. He wants us to be truthful with ourselves, with Him, and with other people:

Rather, let our lives lovingly express truth [in all things, speaking truly, dealing truly, living truly]. Enfolded in love, let us grow up in every way and in all things into Him Who is the Head, [even] Christ (the Messiah, the Anointed One). (Ephesians 4:15)

When we refuse to embrace and love truth, it will prevent spiritual growth. We are held in bondage by what we refuse to face and deal with. Some things are buried so deep that we don't consciously think about them, but like an infection they are eating away at our life: "Who can discern his lapses and errors? Clear me from hidden [and unconscious] faults" (Psalm 19:12).

We are held in bondage by what we refuse to face and deal with.

I walked away from my father's house when I was eighteen years old. I had planned to do so for many years. I knew when I graduated from high school and was able to get a job and be self-supporting that I would leave. It was the only way I knew to get away from the abuse I had endured for so long. I walked away from the problem thinking it was over, yet not realizing I still had the problem in my soul.

I spent years hiding it, refusing to talk about it or even think about it, but that did not prevent me from having problems related to it. The infection was growing daily into something that was gradually taking over my life. The only way to stop it was to expose it. God knew that, and He graciously worked with me through His Holy Spirit to do so. He brought the right people, books, and other material into my hands to help me realize I was not alone in my pain. Thousands of people had experienced abuse at the hands of their parents and other relatives and friends.

The Bible teaches us to confess our faults to one another so that we may be healed and learn to love one another (See James 5:16). My father's abusing me was not a fault in me, but I saw it as one. It had to be dealt with. It had to be exposed in order for me to be an emotionally, mentally, spiritually healthy individual. Actually the stress of hiding the abuse was even affecting my physical health.

Many psychiatrists and psychologists become very successful by letting people talk to them about the things that bother them. They also give advice, but the main service they provide is a listening ear and patient privacy. Everyone needs someone to talk to, someone they feel they can be honest with, someone who won't tell their secrets. If you have trouble accepting yourself, pray and ask God to provide spiritually mature people to be your friends, people you can trust who will listen and understand, but who will also speak truth into your life. Don't just look for someone who will feel sorry for you; you need truth more than pity.

———————— ✥ ————————

Everyone needs someone to talk to, someone they feel they can be honest with.

———————— ✥ ————————

God provided that for me in my husband, but it sure made me angry for many long years. Dave would not come to my "pity parties." He was not mean to me, but he was truthful. I can remember him saying to me, "Joyce, you want me to feel sorry for you, and I am not going to do that because it won't help you." I was trapped in endless rounds of self-pity, and the last thing I needed was someone to feel sorry for me. I thought I wanted pity, but I thank God now that He gave me what I needed, not what I wanted.

Don't get angry at the people God provides to be truthful with you. They should speak the truth in love, but they *should* speak the truth (See Ephesians 4:15 KJV).

A NEW BEGINNING

When people begin studying God's Word and learn how to live in the light and not be afraid of it, their lives change for the better. God knows everything, and He loves you and me anyway, so even if we never find anyone else, we can be totally open and honest with the Lord. He hates pretense, so just be honest. Ask Him to reveal to you anything you may be hiding from or afraid to face— and then buckle your seat belt. You may be in for the ride of your life. It may be a bumpy ride at times, and frightening at others. You may scream, "Stop the ride and let me off; I can't take any more!" But one thing is for sure; it is a ride that will eventually take you where you want to go, which is to a life that you can enjoy, one that bears good fruit for God.

God has revealed so much to me about myself that I am amazed. We think we know ourselves, when in reality we are often hiding, not only from others, but especially from ourselves. God had to show me many things about myself that were very uncomfortable, things I rejected at first, thinking, "I can't be that way." He showed me I was hard to get along with, controlling, manipulative, fearful, insecure, and hard-hearted. I talked too much. I pretended to need nobody, when in reality I was very needy indeed. I acted as tough as a raging lion on the outside, but on the inside I was as weak as a newborn kitten. I blamed my past for everything I did wrong. I made excuses for bad behavior rather than taking responsibility for it. The list is too long to continue, but the good news is that I can now say, "I used to be that way, and I have changed."

As I always say, "I am not where I need to be, but thank God I am not where I used to be. I am okay, and I am on my way!"

Don't be afraid of your weaknesses any longer. Don't allow them to make you hate yourself. Give them all to God, and He will surprise you by using them. Give Him all that you are and especially all that you are not. When you do surrender to God in this way, you will experience a release from those things that burden you. You will be able to live light and free.

———— ☙ ————
Give Him all that you
are and especially all
that you are not.
———— ☙ ————

Don't let your weaknesses and imperfections embarrass you. You are a human being, so give yourself permission to be one. Love yourself in spite of everything you see wrong with yourself. We all have to deal with our little load of faults and imperfections. Yours may not be the same as someone else's, but believe me, they are no worse. You are going to have them anyway, so you may as well give yourself permission to be imperfect. Accept it—you are not perfect, and never will be. So if you are ever going to approve of yourself, you will have to do it in your imperfect state.

ENTERING GOD'S REST CONCERNING YOUR FAULTS

For we who have believed (adhered to and trusted in and relied on God) do enter that rest. (Hebrews 4:3)

I remember when God told me to give myself permission to be weak. It was very hard for me because I truly despised weakness. I thought weak people got walked on. My mother had been weak. She let my dad abuse her verbally, emotionally, and physically. She let him abuse me sexually. She was too weak to deal with it. She didn't know what to do and could not face the scandal. I never hated my mother, but I did grow to hate weakness.

I did not respect people whom I viewed as being weak. As a result, I could not accept weaknesses in myself. I tried to be tough in all situations. The problem was that I did have weaknesses like everyone else, and trying to conquer all of them was creating major stress in my life in addition to ungodly self-hatred and self-rejection. I suffered greatly trying to overcome every flaw I saw in myself. Even when I did succeed at conquering one, I saw two more.

God had told me to give myself permission to have weaknesses. I knew I had heard from God, but it was a major step of faith. I was afraid that if I just accepted weaknesses as a part of life, they would multiply and take over. I had yet to learn that where we stop, God begins. When we cast our care upon Him, He takes our care and carries it for us (See 1 Peter 5:7). Instead of my weaknesses

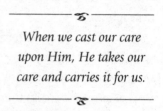

When we cast our care upon Him, He takes our care and carries it for us.

multiplying and taking over my life, God began to strengthen me in them. He began to flow through them. Oh, I knew my weaknesses were still in existence, but even that knowledge caused me to lean on Him constantly. My relationship with Him deepened. I was being honest, I was being dependent, and I needed Him without interruption.

God works in those who believe by making changes on an ongoing basis. In Philippians 1:6 we see He has begun a good work in us, and He intends to finish it and bring it to completion. *The Amplified Bible* translation of this verse says He will be perfecting His work in us right up until Christ returns. If this work is never going to be completely concluded until Jesus calls us home, then why torment ourselves all of our lives? God has given us permission to love ourselves as we are. We can enter His rest concerning what remains to be done in our personalities, character, and life. Believing allows us to enter God's rest.

ALL OF US HAVE A LIMP

Jacob was a man who had many weaknesses, and yet he pressed on with God and was determined to be blessed by Him. God likes that kind of determination. He actually told Jacob he had contended with God and man, and He would be glorified in him (See Genesis 32:28). God can gain glory for Himself through those who will not let their personal weaknesses stop Him from flowing through them.

For God to do that through us, first we must come face to face with the fact that we have weaknesses, and then we must determine not to let them bother us. Our imperfections are not going to stop God unless we let them do so.

I'm going to ask you to do something and it's very important. Stop right now, wrap your arms around yourself, give yourself a big hug, and say out loud: "I accept myself. I love myself. I know I have weaknesses and imperfections, but I will not be stopped by them." Try doing that several times a day, and you will soon develop a new attitude and outlook.

Jacob wrestled with the angel of the Lord who touched the hollow of his thigh, and as a result, he always had a limp from that day forward (See Genesis 32:24–32). I always say that Jacob limped off from the fight, but he limped away with his blessing. Another way to say it is this: "God will bless us even though all of us have a limp (an imperfection)." Remember, God sees our heart. If we have our faith in Him, and a heart that wants to do right, that is all that is needed.

ACCEPT A BLESSING FOR JESUS' SAKE

David and Jonathan had a covenant relationship that included all their heirs (See 1 Samuel 18:3; 20:16; 23:16–18). Jonathan was killed, but David became king and began looking for someone he could bless for Jonathan's sake. God is looking for someone He can bless for Jesus' sake. It can be you, if you will agree.

Jonathan had a son named Mephibosheth who was lame in both feet. He had been living for years in a small town called Lo-debar. It was not a nice town, not a popular town. When our self-image is poor, we often choose surroundings that seem to fit the way we feel about ourselves. I have noticed that some people who are filled with self-loathing won't even bother to fix themselves up or even try to dress or look nice. The way they feel about themselves inside shows on the outside. Other people go to the opposite extreme. They feel so bad about themselves inwardly that they try to hide it by becoming perfectionists outwardly. Everything around them has to appear to be perfect—their homes, personal appearance, children, spouse, et cetera. They live under tremendous pressure, and they also pressure the other people in their lives.

We respond to the same problem in different ways depending on our temperament and background. Mephibosheth responded by hiding and avoiding the very people who could have helped him. He knew he had rights to land and other privileges because of his father Jonathan's covenant relationship with David who was now the king, but he remained poverty stricken and lonely. Why? Because of the way he saw himself. He let his lame feet embarrass him and keep him from demanding his rights.

How many of us do the same thing? We won't pray boldly or even receive the blessings God freely offers because of the way we see ourselves. We assume if we see ourselves in a negative manner, God and everyone else must see us that way too, but that is not true.

The story of Mephibosheth is told in 2 Samuel, chapter 9, and ends by stating that he finally came to the royal palace by invitation from King David. Everything that was rightfully his was restored to him, and he ate at the king's table even though he was lame in both feet (See vv. 7 and 13). You see, people with a limp (imperfections) can still be blessed, but they must realize that their imperfections don't stop God:

> Sing, O Daughter of Zion; shout, O Israel! Rejoice, be in high spirits and glory with all your heart, O Daughter of Jerusalem in that day.
>
> [For then it will be that] the Lord has taken away the judgments against you; He has cast out your enemy. The King of Israel, even the Lord [Himself], is in the midst of you; [and after He has come to you] you shall not experience or fear evil any more.
>
> In that day it shall be said to Jerusalem, Fear not, O Zion. Let not your hands sink down or be slow and listless.
>
> The Lord your God is in the midst of you, a Mighty One, a Savior [Who saves]! He will rejoice over you with joy; He will rest [in silent satisfaction] and in His love He will be silent and make no mention [of past sins, or even recall them]; He will exult over you with singing.
>
> Behold, at that time I will deal with all those who afflict you; *I will save the limping [ones] and gather the outcasts and will make them a praise and a name in every land of their shame.* (Zephaniah 3:14–17, 19, italics mine)

Stop! If you didn't read the Scripture passages above, I am asking you to go back and do so. I know from experience that sometimes when we are reading a book that includes Scripture, we are so interested in what the book says we skip over some of the Scriptures. In this case I highly recommend that you not only read the Scriptures, but that you also digest them.

These Scriptures share the fact that God wants to bless those who would appear to be outcasts, those with "limps" in their life. He has determined to gather them and bless them. He promises to cast out the enemy, who in many cases is shame, blame, and disgrace. God does not want you to experience or fear evil any more. He wants you to rest in peace and enjoy your life. He wants you to enjoy yourself, loving yourself in a balanced way.

God does not want you to experience or fear evil any more.

So take a moment, read the Scriptures, then thank God for loving you as you are and for teaching you how to love yourself. When you are ready, we will move into the second section of this book, in which we'll take what we have learned about self-acceptance and apply it toward some specific battles we need to win to properly deal with the approval addiction. Keep pressing on!

PART

II

Addressing Our
Addictions

Overcoming Approval Addiction

When we think of addicts, we may immediately think of drugs or alcohol. But the truth is we can be addicted to almost anything. The apostle Paul stated that he would not allow anything to control him (See 1 Corinthians 6:12). That is a good attitude to have, one that we will have to be very determined to maintain. Even the most "spiritual" people can become addicted to things. Their addictions may not be the things we ordinarily think of when we hear the word *addict*, but they are real addictions nonetheless.

As we saw earlier, an addiction is something people feel they cannot live without, or something they feel compelled to do in order to relieve pressure, pain, or discomfort of any kind. A drug addict, for example, will do whatever is necessary to get another "fix" whenever he begins to feel uncomfortable. An alcoholic will feel compelled to drink, especially when confronted with life's problems. The substance to which people are addicted helps relieve their pain momentarily, but a controlling cycle begins in their life that is destructive.

I smoked cigarettes for many years and was addicted to nicotine. I experienced the same types of things I have described, thankfully to a lesser degree. For example, if I was in a tense situation, the first thing I reached for was a cigarette. If I became angry or was under stress of any kind, I smoked even more than I normally did. I used smoking to relieve tension rather than dealing with life's problems the way God would have chosen for me. I would certainly not have considered myself an addict, but eventually I had to face the truth that not only was I addicted to cigarettes, but there were other things in my life that were controlling me as well. I was addicted to approval, the need to be in control, work, reasoning, and other things. Since I desired to be able to say with the apostle Paul, "I will not allow anything to control me," I had to be willing to face the truth and allow God to change me.

ADDICTED TO REASONING

God revealed to me that I was addicted to reasoning. I absolutely could not feel comfortable and at peace unless I thought I had everything in my life figured out. I wanted to know what was going to happen, and how and when it was going to take place. If I did not know, I became anxious, restless, nervous, worried, and grouchy.

> *People who worry excessively clearly show they trust themselves, and not God, to solve their problems.*

I experienced symptoms similar to those of a drug addict who needs a "fix"; the degree of severity was not the same, but the symptoms were.

At the time, I was a Christian and part of the "faith movement," meaning that I supposedly walked by faith. Yet in reality that was not true. I trusted

Jesus for my salvation, but in many other areas I trusted myself to provide the answers I needed for daily life.

People who worry excessively clearly show they trust themselves, and not God, to solve their problems. Worry is a sin and should be repented of like any other sin.

In my case, there was always something going on either in my life, or in someone else's that I was "working on" or trying to reason out. I thought of various answers that seemed to make sense, and for a time they comforted me; but things did not usually turn out the way I had figured they would. I recall the Holy Spirit speaking to my heart and saying: "Joyce, you think you have life all figured out. You think you know what I am going to do, and how I am going to do it. But you really don't know much at all. Joyce, you are not half as smart as you think you are."

The Bible tells us not to be wise in our own eyes (See Proverbs 3:7). In other words, "Don't even think you are intelligent enough to run your own life and have answers for everything."

O Lord [pleads Jeremiah in the name of the people], I know that [the determination of] the way of a man is not in himself; it is not in man [even in a strong man or in a man at his best] to direct his [own] steps. (Jeremiah 10:23)

Life would be so much easier if we would believe God's Word and act accordingly, but most of us have to find out what works and what does not the hard way. His Word says we don't have it in us to run our own lives, but we still try.

I didn't enjoy peace because of my reasoning, but I had done it for so long I did not know any other way to live. That is the way addicts are. They don't like their lives, but at the same time they can't face having it any other way. They hate it, but they need it.

When I was growing up, I had to take care of myself from an early age. My parents provided housing, clothing, and things like that, but I felt I was being used rather than loved. I didn't trust anyone, because the people who said they loved me abused me and disappointed me. My father abused me, and my mother abandoned me. She didn't physically leave the home, but she pretended she did not know what was happening to me, when in reality she knew quite well. She was unable to take action to help me because of fear; she was afraid of the scandal a child abuse case might cause. The rejection and abandonment I experienced in my childhood was the root of my approval addiction. I had a deep sense of being flawed, and since I didn't approve of myself, I was afraid no one else approved of me either.

As a child, I never felt safe. I did not feel I could express a need or a desire and expect my parents to meet it. I did not want to ask for anything, especially from my father, because there was always a price to pay. I developed a habit of looking ahead mentally, always trying to stay one step ahead of being needy. I didn't want to need anyone. I determined to take care of myself, which is a huge job for a child. I even determined to take care of others, especially my mother. She did not seem to be able to take care of me and protect me, so I became the "rescuer" in the family. I grew up with a false sense of responsibility. Even today, I must resist the temptation to feel responsible for things other people should be taking care of themselves.

I also became addicted to the need to be in control. I was afraid to let others make any decisions, because I had no confidence they would be concerned for me. I was accustomed to being used. Once I got away from home and could run my own life, I determined that I would never get hurt again. I promised myself, "Nobody will ever take advantage of me again; nobody is going to tell me what to do."

I became rebellious toward authority, especially male authority. I wasn't mean—I was afraid! If I was not in control, I became frantic, trying to manipulate circumstances in such a way that I would always get what I wanted.

There are endless addictions, but let us now discuss "approval addiction."

THE NEED FOR APPROVAL

When we base our self-worth on how people treat us, or on what we believe they think about us, it causes us to become addicted to their approval. We do not have to be approved of by certain individuals in order to feel good about ourselves. When we think we do, we have a false belief that will open the door for a great deal of misery in our lives. We may spend a lot of time and effort trying to please people and gain their approval. But then, if it takes only one glance of disapproval or one unappreciative word to ruin our sense of self-worth, we are in bondage. No matter how hard we work to please people and gain their acceptance, there will always be someone who disapproves of us.

In Galatians chapter 4, the Bible speaks about two covenants, describing two ways in which we can live. Let's take a look at them.

I. THROUGH WORKS OF THE FLESH

The first way we can choose to live is by works of our own flesh. We can take care of ourselves, make our own plans, and struggle to make things happen our way, in our timing. It is the natural way, the normal way that most people live. It is a way that produces every kind of misery. We struggle, get frustrated, fail, and end up weary and worn out most of the time. We are confused, defeated, and have no peace or joy.

2. THROUGH FAITH

The second way we can live is supernaturally, by the power of God. We can live by faith, trusting God to do what needs to be done in our lives. This way is described in the Bible as a "new and living way" (See Hebrews 10:20), which we will examine later in this book. This new way produces peace, joy, ease, and success.

Either we can try to gain acceptance from people the world's way, or we can choose God's way.

SUPERNATURAL FAVOR

> When a man's ways please the Lord, He makes even his enemies to be at peace with him. (Proverbs 16:7)

God will give us favor with people if we ask Him to do so and put our trust in Him. He can cause even our enemies to be at peace with us.

When I first began preaching, I of course wanted people to like and accept me, and I still do. At that time I did not know much about trusting God for supernatural favor, so I felt a lot of pressure to do all the right things in the hope people would accept me and approve of me.

The problem with that type of mind-set is that everyone expects something different, and no matter how hard we try, we cannot please all of the people all the time. Some people felt my conferences were too long, while others wanted me to spend even more time preaching to them. Some thought the music was too loud, while others wanted it louder. Most of the people who attended loved my preaching style, but occasionally someone would be offended by my straightforward approach and send me a letter of correction. Any disapproval would literally make me almost sick with worry and feelings of rejection—until I learned to trust God rather than trying to "earn" acceptance.

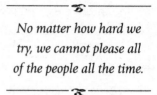

No matter how hard we try, we cannot please all of the people all the time.

In the earlier years of my life, before I allowed God to do a work in me, I did a lot of pretending. Whatever I thought people wanted me to be, that was what I tried to be. I wore many masks, trying to be accepted by everyone. This type of behavior can become a real problem if it is not addressed and changed. God will never help us be anyone other than ourselves.

In *The Mask Behind the Mask,* biographer Peter Evans says that actor Peter Sellers played so many roles he sometimes was not sure of his own identity.[1] In other words, Sellers played so many parts that he forgot who he was. I can remember crying out to God in frustration one day saying, "I don't know who I am or how I am supposed to act." At times I felt like a vending machine. Everyone who came near pushed a different button, expecting a different thing. My husband wanted a good, adoring, submissive wife. My children wanted an attentive mother. My parents and aunt, who are all elderly and dependent on me, wanted my attention. The call on my life demanded many things. The people I ministered to wanted me to be available for them whenever they felt they needed me. I said yes to everything until I finally became sick from stress and realized that if I did not learn to say no, I was in for serious health issues. I wanted everyone to love me and accept me, I desperately wanted their approval, but I was trying to get it the wrong way.

The Lord told me that He would give me favor with people if I would pray for them and trust Him. God can cause people to accept and like us who would normally despise us. The Bible says He changes the hearts of men the way He changes the watercourses (See Proverbs 21:1). If God can make a river flow in a specific direction, surely He can change someone's heart toward us. We wear ourselves out trying to do what only God can do.

God can and will open the right doors for you and give you favor with the right people at the right time.

God can and will open the right doors for you and give you favor with the right people at the right time. For example, God can get you a job that would be far better than anything you could ever get for yourself. Actually, God got me a job I was not even qualified to do, and then enabled me to do it. I worked in a business as a general manager and handled things most people would need a college degree and many years of experience in order to do. At the time I had neither, but God was on my side. We can have favor with God, and He will give us favor with man.

I trust God for favor. When God favors us, He gives us things and does things for us that we do not deserve in the natural. Actually, the job I do now is one I don't deserve and am not naturally qualified for, but one that God daily enables me to do. Jesus said the anointing of the Holy Spirit qualified Him for what He did (See Luke 4:18–19), and it is the same thing that qualifies me for what I do. God has selected and chosen me for this job. He has anointed me.

He wants to do the same thing for all of His children, if they will let Him. Remember, God begins where we end. Stop struggling, trying to make things happen according to your desires, and ask God to take the driver's seat in your life.

As long as we try to make things happen by the works of our flesh, God will stand back and wait for us to wear ourselves out. Eventually we will do just that, and hopefully at that time we will call upon the Lord.

WE CAN'T PLEASE ALL THE PEOPLE ALL THE TIME

Any of us who intend to do very much in life will have to accept the fact that there will be times when we will not receive approval from everyone. The need to be popular will steal our destiny. I deal with and minister to a wide variety of people. There is no way humanly possible that I can please all of them all the time. We have more than five hundred employees at *Joyce Meyer Ministries.* We almost never make one decision that suits all of them.

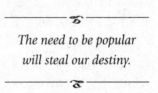

The need to be popular will steal our destiny.

The Bible says Jesus made Himself of no reputation (See Philippians 2:7 KJV). That is a significant statement. He was not well thought of by many people, but His heavenly Father approved of Him and what He was doing, and that was all that really mattered to Him. As long as you and I have God's approval, we have what we need most. The apostle Paul said that if he had been trying to be popular with people, he would not have been a servant of the Lord Jesus Christ (See Galatians 1:10). Paul was saying that needing people's approval in an unbalanced way can steal our destiny. We cannot always be God-pleasers and people-pleasers at the same time.

Pray for favor. Confess that you have favor with God and that He gives you favor with man. Before embarking on any business venture, ask for favor. When you meet new people, ask for favor. I even ask God for favor before going into a restaurant. He can get me the best seat in the house, the best waiter, the best service, and the best food. The Bible says in James 4:2, "You do not have, because you do not ask." Start asking for favor regularly, and you will be amazed at the acceptance and blessings that come your way. You will

> ───────── ✆ ─────────
> *We cannot always be*
> *God-pleasers and people-*
> *pleasers at the same time.*
> ───────── ✆ ─────────

have so many friends you will have to pray about which invitations to take or decline.

Develop your faith in the area of favor. Live expecting it all the time. Remember, you cannot please all the people all the time, but God can give you favor. Trust Him to choose your friends, to open the right doors, and to close the wrong ones. Ask the Lord for "divine connections," friendships that will be perfect for you. God can connect you with people who will add to your life rather than taking away from it.

Even though God gives you favor, you will still encounter times when certain people won't approve of you. Strive to please God, and let Him deal with the people.

BONDAGE OR FREEDOM

As I have mentioned, there are two ways to live. We can live by grace, which is by God's favor and help, or we can live by works, which is by our own efforts, trying to do God's job. One way produces bondage, the other freedom.

Here are some examples. There are two kinds of righteousness:

one that we try to earn by our own perfect record of good works, and one that God gives us through our faith in Jesus Christ.

There are two kinds of love we can have: the love we try to earn and deserve, and the love we receive as a free gift from God.

There are two kinds of love we can give: First is the plain, ordinary kind that people must deserve and earn; when we feel they don't deserve our love, we withhold it. We can also give the love of God, which He has given us. We can let His love flow through us. God's love is an unconditional love. We can receive it from Him and give it away to others.

There are two ways to prosper in life: trying to make our own way and struggling according to the world's system, or doing what God says by tithing all your increase and giving offerings as God leads. When we choose to honor God with our tithes and offerings, He always meets our needs.

There are two kinds of promotion: We can try to promote ourselves, always seeking ways to push ourselves forward, or we can trust God to promote us and give us favor.

There are two kinds of approval: one is from people, and the other is from God. We want people to approve of us, but if we become addicted to their approval, if we have to have it and are ready to do whatever they demand to get it, we lose our freedom. If we trust God for approval, we are freed from the addiction of approval.

BOUNDARIES AND BALANCE OR BURNOUT

Those who are addicted to approval frequently get "burned out." For them there always exists the danger of attempting too much. They so desperately want to please that they do everything they feel is expected of them and then some. They may be committed to being "nice." Sometimes they say yes just because they cannot say no, not because they think their actions are the will of God. They burn out for lack of discernment or because of unwarranted guilt. And so, also, their anger builds.

We become angry when we feel all used up and pulled in every direction. Burnout makes us angry because we recognize deep down inside that it is not normal. We become angry with the people pressuring us, when in reality we are allowing ourselves to be pressured. To avoid pressure from others and from ourselves, we must take control of our lives under the guidance of the Holy Spirit.

Once when I was complaining about my heavy schedule, I heard the Holy Spirit say, "Joyce, you are the one who makes your schedule; if you don't like it, then do something about it."

Frequently we complain and live silently angry lives while at the same time continuing to do the very things that make us angry. It is true people should not pressure us, but it is equally true we should not allow ourselves to come under pressure. We cannot blame others for what is ultimately our own responsibility.

Normal Christian life should be lived within the boundaries of balanced living. Once a person has a serious case of burnout, it is not easy to fix. None of us, not even those of us "called by God," can break His natural laws without paying the penalty. Even though we may work for God, we cannot live without limits. Jesus rested. He walked away from the demands of the crowds and took time for renewal.

Many of God's most precious and well-known saints have suffered from weariness and burnout with a tendency toward depression. We must learn that not all of our problems are spiritual; some of them are physical. We often blame the devil for things that are our own fault. We must learn to say no and not fear the loss of relationships. I have come to the conclusion that if I lose a relationship because I tell someone no, then I really never had a true relationship at all.

RELATIONSHIPS

Relationships are an important part of life. God desires that we have enjoyable, healthy ones. A relationship is not healthy if one person is in control while the other struggles for approval. Nor is it healthy to gain it by being ready to do anything the other party wants, no matter what it is or how that individual feels about it personally. If we have to sin against our own consciences in order to have someone's approval, we are out of the will of God.

I have mentioned that you can buy friends by letting them control you, but you will have to keep them the same way you obtained them. Eventually you will get tired of having no freedom. It is actually better to be lonely than to be manipulated and controlled.

Be careful how you get started in a new relationship. What you allow in the beginning will come to be expected. When we enter business arrangements with new people we have not worked with before, Dave always sets boundaries. If we get a job or product back that is inferior in any

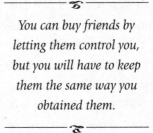

You can buy friends by letting them control you, but you will have to keep them the same way you obtained them.

way, he immediately lets them know that we expect excellence. If they start out being late for appointments and not calling, he lets them know that type of behavior is not acceptable. There have been times when I have thought he was being a little too hard on them, but he always says, "If we don't establish from the beginning what we expect, we will be taken advantage of later."

Just remember that what you allow in the beginning of a relationship should be what you can be happy with permanently. Let people know by your actions that even though you would like their approval, you can live without it if you have to. Respect others, and let them know that you expect them to show you respect also.

Sometimes people compromise in the early stages of a relationship in order to get something or someone they want. They think they can change the person later, but it doesn't always work that way. I know many women who have married unbelievers thinking they could convince them to love Jesus later. Most of them ended up spending their lives being miserable, "unequally yoked with unbelievers" (2 Corinthians 6:14).

Recently I was visiting a friend in Minnesota, and while I was there I met a woman who asked me to elaborate on the meaning of not being "unequally yoked with an unbeliever." She was dating a man who claimed to be a Christian but was not really committed to Christ. She herself had been raised in a Christian home and maintained an active, personal relationship with the Lord. Her father had been aggressively opposed to her continuing the relationship with this man, telling her she would be "unequally yoked."

When we are emotionally attached to someone, we must be very careful not to let our emotions override wisdom and drown out the voice of God. I simply told this woman that she would be making a mistake to marry the man hoping he would change later. If he was a Christian, then he needed to prove it by showing commitment to following a Christian lifestyle.

Many people say they are Christians but show no fruit of it. The Bible says, "You will know them by their fruit" (See Matthew 7:16). Many people mentally accept the existence of God, but that does not mean they are committed to serving Him. The world is actually full of people who believe in God but live in sin.

This woman shared with me that the man she was dating was beginning to go to church with her occasionally and she was hopeful that he would make a serious commitment. I told her to be sure he did so before she married him. I told her not to compromise in the beginning of the relationship, but to be very clear about her expectations.

Wisdom always chooses now what it will be happy with later on. Don't live like there is no tomorrow, because tomorrow always comes.

When we choose the people with whom we think we want to be in relationship—whether work related or personal—we often find later that our choices were not very wise. Ask God to give you "divine connections." He may choose relationships for you that you would never have chosen because you have preconceived ideas about what you want. Learn to look beyond the exterior of people and see their heart. Someone may look good outwardly and be a nightmare to be in relationship with. Another person may not appeal to you at first glance, and yet when you get to know that individual, he or she may turn out to be the best friend you ever had.

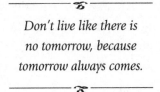

Don't live like there is no tomorrow, because tomorrow always comes.

I was insecure and always wanted to be friends with the "popular people," but quite often I ended up getting hurt. I sought the approval of such people because I was filled with insecurity.

INSECURITY AND APPROVAL ADDICTION

As we discussed in the first part of the book, insecure people easily become approval addicts. They want and need other people's approval so much that they will do just about anything to get it. But security is part of our inheritance from God through Jesus. He wants us to feel safe and comfortable at all times. He wants us to be free to be ourselves and to feel accepted. God will give us that freedom and acceptance through Jesus Christ, if we look to Him for it.

If you have been addicted to approval, or if you know anybody who is, you are aware that it is a miserable way to live. You never know when people are going to approve or disapprove of you. Just about the time you think you have figured out what they want, they may change their mind. You are not free to follow your heart or the leadership of the Holy Spirit because you must always think about what the people want, what will make them happy.

My father was totally dysfunctional. In other words, he did not function the way a father should have. Not only was he abusive in every way, he was impossible to please. Oh, he might show approval occasionally concerning something I had done, yet I could do the same thing at another time and get into trouble for doing it. The atmosphere was terribly unstable and supercharged with fear. It made me feel extremely insecure. I was always afraid of being disapproved of and getting into trouble or being punished. I tried my very best to do what I thought he might want, but it was ever changing and therefore impossible to figure out. Going through this experience eventually turned me into an

> *He wants us to be free to be ourselves and to feel accepted.*

"approval addict"—I so desperately wanted to avoid the pain of disapproval, I was willing to do almost anything to get people's approval.

I had to learn to confront this addiction in my life and confront the people who tried to control me.

CONFRONTATION

Maintaining healthy relationships occasionally requires confrontation. That means you must say no even when the other party wants to hear yes. It means you may have to choose to do something you know the other party won't approve of, if you know it is the right choice for you.

If you have not been confronting, and now find yourself being controlled and manipulated, making a change will not be easy. Once you develop a pattern of pleasing people out of fear, it takes a genuine step of faith to break the pattern.

I was very afraid of my father, and telling him no just didn't seem to be an option. When I left home, I fell into the same pattern with other people who had a personality similar to his. I had difficulty maintaining my freedom, especially with strong-willed people. If I was with someone who would allow it, I became the controller;

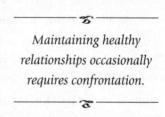

Maintaining healthy relationships occasionally requires confrontation.

however, if the other person had a domineering personality, I always ended up being controlled. True freedom was something foreign to me. I did not know how to give other people freedom, and I did not know how to stand up for my own right to be free.

If people are not accustomed to being confronted, they may

react very aggressively until they become accustomed to the change. You may even need to explain that you realize you have allowed them to have their way in everything in the past, but that you have been wrong. Explain that you have been insecure and have needed their approval, but that now you have to make a change. It will be hard for you and them, but in order to have a healthy relationship, you must do it.

Spend some time praying about it before confronting. Ask God to give you courage. Ask Him to help the other person be willing to change. What is impossible with man is possible with God (See Mark 10:27).

Breaking any addiction will produce suffering, but it leads to victory.

The important thing is to make a decision right now that with God's help you will break the cycle of approval addiction. Initially, you may feel very uncomfortable with the thought that someone is not happy with you, but you must remember your only other choice is spending your life being unhappy. Breaking any addiction will produce suffering, but it leads to victory. We can suffer on our way to victory or we can suffer, in a never-ending cycle of addictions. If you are going to suffer, at least let it be for some worthwhile reason.

In the next chapter I want to look at one of the first obstacles we face when we make the choice to overcome the approval addiction—letting go of the emotional hurts of our past.

CHAPTER

7

Pressing Past the Pain of Feelings

*A*buse, rejection, abandonment, betrayal, disappointment, judgment, criticism, et cetera, all cause pain in our lives. Emotional pain is often more devastating than physical pain. A pain pill or other medication may alleviate physical pain, but emotional pain is not so easy to deal with. Most people are more comfortable talking about their physical pain than their emotional pain. It seems people feel they have to hide emotional pain and pretend it isn't real, or they may even feel guilty for having it. There exists an imbedded idea in people's minds that those with "emotional problems" are second-rate citizens. We can be physically sick and everyone feels sorry for us, but if we have emotional problems we are viewed suspiciously. Our emotions are part of our makeup, and they can wear out or become sick like any other part of the anatomy.

If you have an emotional wound in your life, Jesus wants to heal you. Don't make the mistake of thinking He is only interested in your spiritual life. Jesus can heal you everywhere you hurt!

The root cause of an approval addiction is usually an emotional wound. The Bible teaches us that Jesus came to heal our wounds and bind up and heal our broken hearts, to give us beauty instead of ashes, and the oil of joy to replace mourning (See Isaiah 61:1–3). According to these Scriptures, He also came to open the prison and the eyes of those who are bound. Being addicted to approval is a prison, and I pray that this book is beginning to open your eyes.

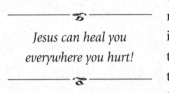

*Jesus can heal you
everywhere you hurt!*

We cannot deal with what we don't recognize and understand, but once our eyes are opened we can learn to enjoy the freedom Jesus desires for each of us.

MAKING RIGHT CHOICES

We have to start making right choices while we are still hurting, which is difficult and painful. Since that is the case, some people never break free. We often have to do the right thing for a long time before we begin getting right results. We must do right and keep doing right, pressing past how we feel about it. For example, treating someone right who has hurt us in the past is emotionally and mentally painful. It seems downright unfair and even like a stupid thing to do. After all, why should we be good to someone who has hurt us? Well, if we cannot find any other reason, we can choose to do it just because Jesus told us to (See Matthew 5:38–44).

If someone has hurt me, and I am bitter about it, that person is in actuality still hurting me. Bitterness is a pain in itself. It is a negative attitude that steals joy and peace. However, if I am willing to press past the pain and make a decision to forgive, I will be free.

If my husband, Dave, hurts my feelings or disappoints me in some way, it
hurts. As long as I refuse to forgive him,
it keeps hurting. As soon as I choose
to do what the Bible teaches me to
do, which is to forgive and treat him
as if nothing happened (See Matthew

*We often have to do the
right thing for a long time
before we begin getting
right results.*

6:14–15), I am free. To be free from the pain, I have to press past it; I
have to choose to do the right thing *while* I am still hurting.

Let me tell you a story that illustrates this point. The scene is a
courtroom trial in South Africa:

A frail black woman about seventy years old slowly rises to her
feet. Across the room and facing her are several white police officers. One of them is Mr. Van der Broek, who has just been tried
and found implicated in the murders of both the woman's son and
her husband some years before. Van der Broek had come to the
woman's home, taken her son, shot him at point blank range and
then set the young man's body on fire while he and his officers par-
tied nearby.

Several years later, Van der Broek and his men had returned for
her husband as well. For months she knew nothing of his where-
abouts. Then almost two years after her husband's disappearance,
Van der Broek came back to fetch the woman herself. How well she
remembers in vivid detail that evening, going to a place beside a
river where she was shown her husband, bound and beaten, but still
strong in spirit, lying on a pile of wood. The last words she heard
from his lips as the officers poured gasoline over his body and set
him aflame were, "Father, forgive them . . ."

Now the woman stands in the courtroom and listens to the con-
fessions offered by Mr. Van der Broek. A member of South Africa's
Truth and Reconciliation Commission turns to her and asks, "So

what do you want? How should justice be done to this man who has so brutally destroyed your family?"

"I want three things," begins the old woman calmly, but confidently. "I want first to be taken to the place where my husband's body was burned so that I can gather up the dust and give his remains a decent burial."

She paused, then continued. "My husband and son were my only family. I want secondly, therefore, for Mr. Van der Broek to become my son. I would like for him to come twice a month to the ghetto and spend a day with me so that I can pour out on him whatever love I still have remaining in me." She also stated that she wanted a third thing, "This is also the wish of my husband. And so, I would kindly ask someone to come to my side and lead me across the courtroom so that I can take Mr. Van der Broek in my arms and embrace him and let him know that he is truly forgiven." As the court assistants came to lead the elderly woman across the room, Mr. Van der Broek, overwhelmed by what he had just heard, fainted. As he did, those in the courtroom, family, friends, neighbours—all victims of decades of oppression and injustice—began to sing, softly but assuredly, "Amazing grace, how sweet the sound, that saved a wretch like me."[1]

Although it appears that the elderly woman who had endured such a painful loss was doing Mr. Van der Broek a huge favor—and indeed she was—she actually was doing more for herself than for him. Because of her actions, her past had no authority over her future. She was not allowing the pain of the past to poison her attitude. Her attitude gave God glory.

God is not glorified by our suffering, but He is glorified when we have a good attitude during suffering. I am sure the woman had to discipline her feelings. She had to make a choice that was not easy, but the reward was worth it. She made a right decision while she was still hurting, and that decision contributed to putting an end to her pain. As long as we stay angry, we keep our pain. When we begin to pray for and bless those who have hurt us, the

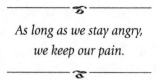

As long as we stay angry, we keep our pain.

pain is swallowed up in love. As Mahatma Gandhi once said, "The weak can never forgive. Forgiveness is the attribute of the strong."

DISCIPLINE IS REQUIRED

The Bible says no discipline for the present seems joyous; nevertheless, later on it will yield the peaceful fruit of righteousness to those who are trained by it (See Hebrews 12:11). Righteousness, or doing what is right, is a fruit that yields peace in our lives. Nothing feels better than simply knowing we did what was right. To me, nothing is worse than a guilty conscience.

When confronted with pain, there are only three choices: (1) press past the pain now, (2) press past the pain later, or (3) keep the pain forever.

The Bible says discipline is sometimes painful. The very thought of the word *discipline* means we will have to choose to do something we don't really feel like doing. If we feel like doing something, discipline is not required or needed.

I don't have to discipline myself to shop for new clothes because I like to do it. However, I know a woman who hates shopping, and she waits until everything she has to wear is seriously outdated or totally worn out before she will go shopping. She has to discipline herself to shop because she does not have feelings supporting her. My feelings support me greatly; therefore, I need no discipline to shop. I must discipline myself *not* to shop at times!

My husband, Dave, loves to exercise. He has been exercising since he was sixteen years old. I hate exercise. My motto is "No pain! No pain!" I like the benefit of exercise, but I don't like to do it. I don't feel like exercising, so I have to press past the pain in order to do it. Exercise for me requires discipline.

We must press past the emotional pain of a lack of desire to do things we don't enjoy. In the same way, we must also press past the emotional pain of abuse, rejection, disapproval, betrayal, judgment, and criticism in order to be set free from them.

Don't allow your past to ruin your future. Why should you remain bitter, angry, and wounded while those who hurt you are out having a good time, not even knowing or caring that you are hurting?

God shows us in His Word how we can be free, but we still have to make choices that may not always be easy or even seem fair.

YOU ARE NOT THE ONLY ONE

The Bible reminds us in 1 Peter 5:9 that we are to stand firm in faith against the attacks of the devil, knowing that identical sufferings are appointed to our brothers and sisters throughout the world.

We all get hurt at times, and we all have the same opportunity either to let it make us bitter or to let it make us better. How can injustices make us better? For one thing, they help us develop character. Doing what is right when we don't have feelings supporting us builds strong character in us. Intelligence and talents are God's gifts, but character is developed. Many people have gifts that can take them to high places, but they don't have the character to keep them there once they arrive.

Not only does everyone get hurt, we all get hurt again and again. That may not sound very encouraging, but it is true. I can recall an occasion in which God was really dealing with me about trusting my husband and his decisions more than I had done in the past. Dave loves me and would never hurt me on purpose, but he is also human and therefore fallible. So I said to God, "What if he hurts me?" The Lord replied, "He probably will from time to time, but I am your Healer. I live inside of you, and I am always available to heal your wounds."

> *Intelligence and talents are God's gifts, but character is developed.*

We spend so much time trying not to get hurt that we cannot develop good relationships with people. We should not spend all of our time trying to protect ourselves. We should be willing to give ourselves away, and lay down our lives for others (See John 15:13).

We may look at other people and think they never have to go through anything difficult, but we all go through different things. Some people have gone through devastating things that nobody knows anything about. They go to God's throne with their problems instead of the phone. Some people have learned the art of suffering silently. They know only God can help them, so they don't bother telling everyone they meet what they are going through.

It is not wrong to share our troubles with a friend or counselor, but the point is that we cannot assume others are not having challenges in life just because they don't look depressed or don't talk about their problems.

My husband rarely ever talks about anything he is going through. There have been times when I have had a virus of some sort and told Dave I was feeling bad, aching all over, nauseated, et cetera. When I did that, he sometimes replied, "I had that three weeks ago. I felt really bad for seven days." I asked him why he didn't tell me he was sick, to which he replied, "Why should I tell you how bad I feel? You can't do anything for me."

Some of us are talkers, and some are not. Don't make the mistake of thinking people have no pain just because they have not told you about it. I believe it is important for us not to think we are the only ones hurting. Peter reminded the people to whom he was writing to resist the devil, knowing everybody was going through the same kind of things they were (See 1 Peter 5:8–9).

> *It is important for us not to think we are the only ones hurting.*

Remembering this truth keeps us from feeling alone and isolated in our own pain. It helps me when I am hurting to remember that somewhere, someone is hurting much worse than I am and I should be grateful I don't have worse problems than I do. I am not alone, and with God's help I will make it through my difficulty. This too shall pass!

THE PROMISE OF REWARD

The promise of reward helps us press past the pain of obedience:

> Instead of your [former] shame you shall have a twofold recompense; instead of dishonor and reproach [your people] shall rejoice in their portion. Therefore in their land they shall possess double [what they had forfeited]; everlasting joy shall be theirs.
>
> For I the Lord love justice. (Isaiah 61:7–8)

And I will restore or replace for you the years that the locust has eaten—the hopping locust, the stripping locust, and the crawling locust, My great army which I sent among you.

And you shall eat in plenty and be satisfied and praise the name of the Lord, your God, Who has dealt wondrously with you. And My people shall never be put to shame. (Joel 2:25–26)

These are two of many wonderful promises in the Bible. God is "the rewarder of those who earnestly and diligently seek Him" (Hebrews 11:6). If we are to be diligent, then we must do what is right when we feel like it and when we don't. The Word of God shares many accounts of men and women who received difficult instructions from the Lord with the promise of reward if they chose to obey.

Esther was asked to do a difficult thing and promised the reward of saving a nation if she would do it (See the book of Esther). Abraham was instructed to leave home and family and go to a place that God would later show him. God told him that his reward would be exceedingly great (See Genesis 12:1–4; 15:1). Joseph was given a dream of being a great ruler, but he had to press past the pain of being rejected and hated by his brothers. He endured thirteen years in prison for a crime he did not commit and kept a good attitude all the while. Even in prison Joseph continued to help other people. He did eventually get his promised reward. He was given a position in Egypt that was second only to Pharaoh himself. During a famine he was able to use his influence to save many people, as well as his family who had hurt him. Joseph had an excellent attitude, and God rewarded him for it (See Genesis 37–50).

Viktor Frankl made the following statement:

We who lived in concentration camps can remember the men who walked through the huts comforting others, giving away their last piece of bread. They may have been few in number, but they offer sufficient proof that everything can be taken from a man but one thing; the last of the human freedoms—to choose one's attitude in any given set of circumstances.[2]

There is no danger of developing eyestrain from looking on the bright side of things, so why not try it?

There is no danger of developing eyestrain from looking on the bright side of things, so why not try it? Being negative only makes a difficult journey more difficult. You may be given a cactus, but you don't have to sit on it.

Doing the right thing—letting go of the emotional pain—when we are getting immediate results is not very challenging, but continuing to do so when it seems that nothing right is happening to us is very challenging indeed. All of these people I just mentioned had to endure in order to receive their promised reward.

THE PAIN OF DISAPPROVAL

All those who are addicted to approval feel emotional and mental pain when they experience disapproval. In order to break free from approval addiction they must press past the pain they feel when they experience disapproval. Approval addicts attempt to avoid or relieve the pain of disapproval by doing whatever people want them to do. Let me give you an example of what I mean.

A young woman I know—I'll call her Jenny—is addicted to approval. Her mother has always been very difficult to please, and

Jenny has felt the pain of rejection many times in her life. Like any child, she wants her mother's approval, which is a very normal desire.

Jenny has fallen into the trap of "people-pleasing" in her relationship with her mother, who is a very controlling individual. Her mother expects Jenny to drop whatever she may be doing in order to cater to her every whim. She becomes angry if Jenny has already made plans and is unable to take her places or help her with projects. Jenny's mother is quite unreasonable, but Jenny's approval addiction not only keeps her miserable, it also feeds her mother's addiction to control.

In order to have freedom and be able to enjoy her life and her mother, Jenny will have to choose to do what she knows is right for her, even if it means that her mother will disapprove. She must be willing to endure the pain of rejection. Every time she relieves her pain by giving in to her mother, she feeds her addiction as well as her mother's.

You can starve an addiction to death by simply not feeding it. Don't fight with addictions, but instead refuse to feed them.

The decision not to give in will be hard for Jenny emotionally, because she has always caved in and let her mother have her way. It won't be easy for Jenny's mother either, because she is addicted to getting what she wants. She needs to be in control in order to feel good about herself.

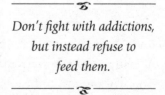

Don't fight with addictions, but instead refuse to feed them.

Do you see the trap Satan sets for people? Jenny needs approval, and her mother needs control. Jenny's mother's problem controls Jenny, and Jenny's problem feeds her mother's. Each time Jenny says no and sticks with her decision, the pain and discomfort she experiences will lessen. It might be compared to a diet. If a person indulges himself and overeats for a long period of time, his capacity for food is increased. Should he decide to cut down on his eating, he will feel the pain of hunger the first few days he decreases his food intake. However, each day that goes by in which he sticks to his decision to eat less, he will feel less discomfort until eventually he will be able to eat less and not feel uncomfortable at all.

The same principle applies to any area of life that needs to be disciplined. Anything we are accustomed to having, we want. If we don't get it, we feel discomfort until we get used to doing without it.

Jenny will have to endure some difficulty for a period of time. At times her difficulty will seem to be more than she can stand, but if she refuses to go back to being controlled by her mother, eventually she will be free, and Jenny and her mother hopefully will be able to begin developing a new and healthy relationship. If Jenny and her mother are both willing, they can indeed start afresh.

BREAKING THE CYCLE OF ADDICTION

I want to encourage you to replace one addiction with another one. You are probably thinking, "What sense does that make?" Actually, I want you to replace all addictions with one other addiction. I want you to become addicted to Jesus! You should need Him more than you need anything else.

I mentioned that for Jenny there might be times when she will feel that her pain and discomfort are more than she can stand. What is she to do during those times? She needs to run quickly to the Lord—to His Word and promises. If she will study select portions of Scripture that strengthen and encourage her, she will be enabled to do the right thing.

God's Word has inherent power in it. When we release our faith in His Word, that power is released into our lives and situations to help us.

Jenny should also pray during these times. She should pray specifically for strength not to give in to her mother's demands but rather to stand firm in the will of God.

She should not only pray during these times, she should also pray ahead of time in these areas.

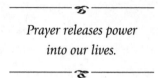

Prayer releases power into our lives.

I have learned to pray regularly in areas that I know to be weaknesses for me. Too often we wait until we are in the midst of a temptation and find the pressure of it to be more than we can resist. Jesus said that we are to pray that we come not into temptation (Luke 22:40). We will be tempted, but if we pray regularly and prior to the times of temptation as well as in them, we will find ourselves enjoying more victory. Prayer releases power into our lives.

Determination and discipline are important in breaking the cycle of addictions, but receiving supernatural strength from God is the real key to success. Learn to run to Him instead of running to the substance or wrong behavior to which you are addicted.

I have spent so many years seeking God every morning that now I just don't feel right unless I have my daily time with Him. I actually get grouchy and act impatiently throughout the day if I don't feed on His Word and spend time in His presence. In the 1970s when I began developing a habit of spending daily time with God, it was hard to do. Other things always came up. I could not concentrate. I even got bored. But, after years of giving God a place of priority in my time, I am addicted to it. Now I am uncomfortable if I don't have it.

Every unhealthy addiction can be broken in your life. You can live a balanced, joy-filled, peaceful life if you will lean on God in everything and for everything. He is your Strength. You cannot defeat your "Goliaths" without His help. When David went against the giant Goliath he knew he had to go in the name of the Lord. He told Goliath, "This day the Lord will deliver you into my hand" (1 Samuel 17:46). David knew he could not deliver himself, so he put his trust in God. That is what you must do, especially when faced with the giant of your addiction.

SET YOUR MIND AND KEEP IT SET

The Bible says we are to set our minds, and keep them set, on things above, not on things on the earth (See Colossians 3:2). Having been addicted to approval, I know how difficult it is not to think about it when we feel someone is not pleased with us. Thoughts of that person's anger and rejection seem to fill our every waking moment.

Instead of trying not to think wrong thoughts, choose right ones. Fill your mind with positive thoughts. Meditate on God's Word and His will for you. Then wrong thoughts will find no place of entry.

We have all had the experience of being terribly worried about something, of having our minds rotating around and around a problem endlessly. If we get involved in something else that interests us, we stop worrying for a period of time. When it is quiet and we are alone, or when we have nothing else to do, we begin to worry again. I have found that one of the best allies against wrong

thinking is to stay busy doing something for someone else. I don't have
time to think about "me" when I am
occupied with someone else's need.
In this way I set my mind on what is
above, not on earthly things. I set my

*We must be armed with
right thinking, or we will
give up during hard times.*

mind on God's instruction to me to walk in love (See Ephesians 5:2).

We must be armed with right thinking, or we will give up during hard times:

> So, since Christ suffered in the flesh for us, for you, arm yourselves
> with the same thought and purpose [patiently to suffer rather than
> fail to please God]. For whoever has suffered in the flesh [having the
> mind of Christ] is done with [intentional] sin [has stopped pleasing
> himself and the world, and pleases God]. (1 Peter 4:1)

Realize (set your mind) and be fully aware that moving from
being a victim to being a victor will not be a quick process. It will
take time, but the investment will be worth it in the end. Remember, you can either go through the pain of deliverance that is tem-
porary, or keep the pain of bondage that never ends unless it is
confronted.

DO IT AFRAID

Fear is involved in approval addiction: the fear of rejection, abandonment, being alone, and of what people will think or say about
us. Fear is not from God:

> For God did not give us a spirit of timidity (of cowardice, of craven
> and cringing and fawning fear), but [He has given us a spirit] of

power and of love and of calm and well-balanced mind and discipline and self-control. (2 Timothy 1:7)

Fear means to run away from something. God does not want us
to run from things. He wants us to confront things, knowing that
He has promised to be with us, never to leave us nor forsake us
(See Hebrews 13:5).

There are times in life when we must do things afraid. In other
words, we must do what we know we should do even though we
feel fear. Fear is a spirit that produces feelings and creates physio-
logical changes. Fear can make the heart beat faster and harder. It
can cause sweating, shaking, irrational thinking, and other physical manifestations. The Bible never tells us that we are not to feel
any of those things connected with fear; it simply tells us not to
fear. When God said to people "fear not," He meant for them to
keep going forward, taking steps of obedience to carry out His
instructions to them. He was in essence telling them, "This is not
going to be easy, but don't run away from it." Mark Twain said,
"Courage is resistance to fear, mastery of fear, not absence of fear."
In other words, there are too many people praying for mountains
of difficulty to be removed when what they really need to be praying for is the courage to climb them. Courage is being the only one
who knows you are afraid.

Running from hard things is one of our biggest problems. We try
to avoid the pain and discomfort of fear. Fear has torment (See 1
John 4:18 KJV), and it is a painful thing. We must press past the
pain and do what fear demands that we run from. As French
author Michel de Montaigne once said, "He who fears he shall suffer, already suffers what he fears."

Approval addicts are afraid of the pain of rejection. They will
spend their lives keeping other people happy and fixed while for-

feiting their own joy unless they make a decision to break the cycle of addiction. They will have to "do it afraid." They will have to follow the leading of the Holy Spirit and their own heart rather than following the will and desires of other people.

When I became aware of this principle that I call "Do it afraid," it was life changing for me. I always wanted the feelings of fear to go away, but my desire was unrealistic.

Satan regularly uses fear to prevent us from making progress. He will not stop attacking us with feelings of fear, but we can "fear not." We can "do it afraid." The only way out is through!

The time came in my journey of healing for me to confront my father about the years of abuse I had endured at his hands. I was so afraid I felt as if I might actually faint or my legs might buckle underneath me, but I knew I had to be obedient to God's instruction to confront. Nobody had ever confronted the abuse in our family. We had all just pretended that we were a normal, well-adjusted, loving family. Nobody ever talked about it; we just hid from the truth, and it was destroying all of us.

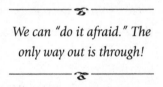

We can "do it afraid." The only way out is through!

Feelings buried alive never die; they just eat away at our mental, emotional, physical, and spiritual health. They also have a devastating effect on the development of healthy relationships. We may hide painful memories, but they are still somewhere doing their dirty work.

As I stood in front of my father and began trying to talk to him about what he had done to me in my childhood, the fear I felt was absolutely horrible. He began reacting in anger and denial. He even started blaming me. At the same time my mother was yelling, crying, and having a major anxiety attack.

I thank God that He gave me the strength to press on rather than run away and hide again. Many years have passed since that day, but it opened the door for true healing. It was a process that involved many stages. The final stage was my father's salvation. He caused me a lot of pain in my life, but I had the joy of baptizing him after leading him into a personal relationship with Christ. If I had not "done it afraid" when God instructed me to confront him, we would still be where we were then. We cannot make progress without confrontation.

I knew a man who was having major chest pains. He was afraid that if he went to the doctor he would find out he had heart trouble, so he ignored the pain, hoping it would go away. He died a short time later! The thing he feared came upon him.

God's Word tells us that we can have what we believe (See Mark 11:22–24), but we can also have what we fear.

THE PAIN OF LONELINESS

The pain of rejection is connected to the pain of being lonely. Loneliness is one of the biggest problems in people's lives today. It is the root cause of many suicides as well as a great deal of personal agony.

Being with people does not guarantee we will not be lonely. We can be with people and still feel lonely because we feel we are misunderstood, that we are not making a connection with those around us. We may be inside a room with people, but we can still feel outside the group.

We must press past the pain of being lonely and feeling misunderstood. We must trust God for right relationships and not make emotional decisions that only end up making our problem worse.

The fear of being lonely can turn us into people-pleasers, and we can end up with no life of our own, bitter and feeling all used up by other people.

Being alone does not constitute being lonely. If you know who you are in Christ, and you like yourself, you can enjoy being alone. I like to spend time with myself because I like myself. Some people have been critical of me for saying, "I like myself." They think I am full of pride. That is not the case at all.

I don't like myself because I think I am wonderful. I like myself because Jesus loves me, and He is wonderful! I like myself because I made a decision to do so, not because I always feel like-able or lovable. As we discussed in chapter 5, I finally decided if Jesus loved me enough to die for me, the very least I could do was stop hating and rejecting myself.

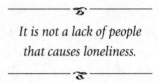

It is not a lack of people that causes loneliness.

When I made this decision, I started enjoying my time alone. Prior to that decision, it seemed I felt lonely no matter how many people I was with. I think loneliness is a result of not liking ourselves more than it is of not having people around us.

Any of us who want to be with people can be. All we have to do is go find others who need help and help them. Hurting people are everywhere. All of us can find someone to do something for, if we really want to. It is not a lack of people that causes loneliness; it is our fears about ourselves as well as our fear of disapproval and rejection.

We frequently spend more time trying to avoid rejection than we do trying to build good relationships. We may be so afraid of being hurt that we keep all of our walls up in an effort to protect ourselves and avoid emotional pain.

Some people isolate themselves. They think they cannot get hurt if they don't get involved, but the result is that they are lonely. Many people are afraid to trust. They are afraid to be honest and vulnerable, afraid that people will judge and criticize them or tell their secrets if they share anything of a private or personal nature. All of these fears and concerns only add to the feelings of loneliness that many people experience. In fact, these fears are the root cause of loneliness.

As human beings, we have a deep need to be understood. When we don't receive it, we feel lonely. In listening to people share their hurt and pain, I find that the words "I understand" have a very soothing effect. I have told my husband, "Even if you don't have a clue about what I am talking about, just tell me you understand, and it will make me feel a lot better." A man could not possibly understand PMS, but it is better for him if he appears to have understanding of his wife's plight. She needs to be understood. She does not want to feel alone in her pain and struggle.

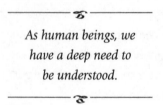

As human beings, we have a deep need to be understood.

One day my husband came in from trying to play golf. He had not had a good experience because his leg was hurting and swollen. He was not too happy about it. His golf game is really important to him, so I said, "I understand how you feel." I offered him whatever help I could give physically, but my understanding seemed to help more than anything.

There have been times in the past when my attitude has been, "What's the big deal? It's only one round of golf. After all, you play all the time." That attitude has started arguments and driven a wedge between us. He wants me to understand his needs, and I want him to understand mine.

One of my favorite Scriptures in the Bible is Hebrews 4:15, which teaches that Jesus is a High Priest Who understands our weaknesses and infirmities because He has been tempted in every respect just as we have, yet He never sinned. Just knowing that Jesus understands makes me feel closer to Him. It helps me be vulnerable and trust Him. It helps me feel connected rather than lonely.

Press past your pain to victory. Be determined! Stop just wishing things were different and do your part to make them different. There are two types of people in the world: those who wait for something to happen, and those who make something happen. We cannot do anything apart from God, but we can decide to cooperate with Him. We can face the truth. We can stop feeding our addictions and endure the pain of letting them die from lack of nourishment.

It is time for a change! Get excited about your future and realize that when you are going through something, the good news is "you're going through," and that means ultimately you will come out on the other side with a victory that cannot be taken away from you. Your experience will make you stronger and enable you to help others who are facing similar battles.

Now let's take a look at what it means to let go of any shame in our past that feeds our approval addiction.

Pressing Past Guilt and Shame

At the age of thirty-three, Christine Caine suddenly discovered she had been adopted. It was quite shocking to her because she had absolutely no inkling of it. Nothing had ever been said in her family that would even remotely indicate she had been adopted.

When she received paperwork from the government regarding the adoption, she found some terminology that wounded her emotionally. She found that she had been "unnamed." A letter actually said she was "unwanted." Her birth mother did not want her and did not name her. At the same time, she was trying to minister to youth, and the university where she applied for further study said she was "unqualified."

Many people who suddenly discovered that they were adopted, unnamed, unwanted, and unqualified for a position they desired would have been devastated and felt guilt and shame, but not Christine. She had been taught God's Word and knew who she was in Christ. She said, "Before God formed me in my mother's womb (whose ever womb that was) He knew me and approved of me as

His chosen instrument" (See Jeremiah 1:5). She made a decision to press past her feelings and live in what she knew to be the truth based on God's Word. She has gone on to become a popular evangelist with a growing worldwide ministry.

Christine could have made another decision. She could have decided to go with the flow of her feelings, which would have pulled her down. She could have felt all the things those words described: unwanted, unqualified, unloved! She could have felt ashamed that her birth mother actually said she did not want her. She could have spent her entire life addicted to approval and living to please people simply because her birth mother had rejected her. She could have felt guilty, as most people do who don't receive affirmation from the people who are supposed to love them. Thank God she decided to press past all the negative feelings and believe God's promises. In the Bible, the psalmist says, "Although my father and my mother have forsaken me, yet the Lord will take me up [adopt me as His child]" (Psalm 27:10).

It is easy to sit in church and say amen when a teacher or preacher shares that we should remain confident in all situations. It is another thing entirely to apply the message when we have a need in our own life. It is easy to agree with the message if we have no feelings that are pushing us to do the wrong thing. To apply

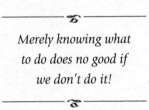

Merely knowing what to do does no good if we don't do it!

God's Word, we must go beyond our feelings and take action based on the truth of His Word.

Christine had spent years in church. She knew a great deal of the Bible and was teaching it to others. She made a decision to apply it to her situation. Once when I was having a serious problem I asked God what I should do, and He told me to do whatever I would tell someone else who came to me for help and had the same problem I now had. Merely knowing what to do does no good if we don't do it!

Christine acted on the Word of God and was rescued from what could have been devastating news. Her adoptive parents had not been truthful with her. She made a decision to be understanding, believe the best, and not resent them for not telling her she was adopted. She found her birth mother and discovered that she lived in her neighborhood only a few blocks from where Christine had lived most of her life. She tried to make contact with her and was told her birth mother wanted absolutely nothing to do with her. This was a major testing time in Christine's life. All she had learned was being put to the test, and she found that God was faithful.

Christine received strength from the Holy Spirit and was able to remain confident. She knew she had worth and value because God loved her. Perhaps she had been unnamed by her mother, but God says in His Word, "Fear not, for I have redeemed you [ransomed you by paying a price instead of leaving you captives]; *I have called you by your name*; you are Mine" (Isaiah 43:1, italics mine).

> *People are much more impressed by our actions than by our words.*

God had a plan for Christine. She was not a mistake; she had been chosen by Him. His anointing qualified her for whatever He called her to do. Because she believed God's Word, the devil was defeated in his plan of destruction. He had hoped that the news of her past would devastate her and create in her an uncontrolled need for acceptance and approval, but it actually strengthened her and others with whom she has shared her story.[1]

People are much more impressed by our actions than by our words. Christine proved by her actions that she really believed what she taught. Her stability in her time of trial continues to encourage others that they need not be defeated by disappointments and what the world would call "bad news." The gospel of Jesus Christ is good news. It is so good that it will overcome all the bad news anyone might ever hear.

SHAME AND BLAME

Because my father sexually abused me, I felt shame, which I internalized. At some point I made an unhealthy transition in my thinking. I was no longer ashamed of what he had done to me; instead, I became ashamed of myself because of it. I took the blame on myself and felt there must be something wrong with me if my own father wanted to do those things to me that I knew were very wrong and unnatural. For years I had a message playing over and over in my mind that said, "What is wrong with me? What is wrong with me? What is wrong with me?" That was one reason I was so excited to learn that I am the righteousness of God in Christ (See 2 Corinthians 5:21). For almost forty years I felt wrong, and now I finally feel right. It is God's will that we feel right about ourselves, not wrong.

My life was literally poisoned with shame. To be shamed can in some cases be defined as being confused, disappointed, or confounded. Confounded can mean defeated, overthrown, or damned. To be damned of course means to be doomed to punishment. Therefore, if people have a shame-based nature, the result is they are doomed to punishment. The bad feelings they have about themselves act as a punishment in itself. When we live every day of our lives not liking ourselves, we are being punished, even if we are the ones doing the punishing.

Like Christine, I was eventually able to learn God's Word and apply it to my situation. But, until I did so, I was miserable. I walked away from my situation when I was eighteen years old, thinking it was all over and done with. As I mentioned previously, I did not realize until later that even though I walked away from the situation that had caused the problem, I still had the problem in my soul.

The important thing in life is what goes on in us: our thoughts, imaginations, attitudes, and inner feelings. The things in us eventually come out one way or another. We may think we have them hidden away where nobody can ever find them, but that is not true.

I was seeing the results of my childhood abuse every day; I just did not know that was what I was seeing. I blamed a lot of my problems on other people and situations. I ran from my problems when I was eighteen, and through blame I had discovered a new way to keep running from them.

THE BLAME GAME

Do not let yourself be overcome by evil, but overcome (master) evil with good. (Romans 12:21)

Blaming others for our own unhappiness only helps us avoid dealing with the real problem. I have finally realized that nobody is responsible for my personal happiness. I tried to make my husband responsible, blaming him every time I did not feel happy. I blamed circumstances, my father and mother, the devil, and even God. The result was that I remained unhappy. As British author Douglas Adams once said, "When you blame others you give up your power to change." If you could kick in the pants the person responsible for most of your trouble, you wouldn't sit for a month. Start taking responsibility for your actions and reactions, and you will start to change.

Through blaming I was avoiding dealing with the real issues that needed to be confronted in my life. I had an infection inside me—not an infection in my physical body, but one in my soul. It was spreading and affecting more and more of my thoughts, attitudes, conversations, and decisions. It was actually affecting my entire outlook on life.

It was time to stop running. As a Christian, I talked about "the promised land," but I lived in the "wilderness." I was like the Israelites of old who traveled around and around in the desert with Moses. They spent forty years attempting to complete a journey that should have taken eleven days (See Deuteronomy 1:2). Why? Among other things they always blamed Moses and God for their difficulties. They never took responsibility for their actions. Everything that went wrong was someone else's fault. They never accepted their own guilt.

I had been abused, and that was not my fault. It was true that I had some problems that were a direct result of the abuse I had suffered; but what I needed was to stop using it as an excuse not to change. Blame keeps us trapped in our problems. We can feel bitter, but we never get any better. I was occupied with thoughts of what people had done to me when I should have been busy praying about what I could do for them or others. God's Word says that we are to overcome evil with good.

Hurting people hurt people. Someone had hurt my father, and he hurt me; blaming him would not change that fact. He was responsible, but that was between him and God to work out. It was not my job to try to make him pay for his mistakes.

Blaming others is a sick game the devil plays with our thoughts and emotions. But if we join in and play the game, only the devil wins—we never win! If we get close to facing any issue, he tries to show us someone or something else we can blame. He wants to divert our attention and momentarily take pressure off of us by giving us yet another reason why nothing is our fault. Don't play his game!

People with a shame-based nature like to place blame. It diverts their attention from the way they feel about themselves for a period of time. The shame of the past is painful and hard to look at. But, hiding from the truth does not mean that it does not exist. It does, in fact, exist and will continue to cause problems until it is confronted and dealt with. Get a grip and face reality; it will be the beginning of the end of your problems.

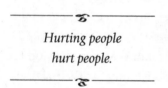

Hurting people hurt people.

I resented the fact that my childhood had been stolen. I never had the privilege of just being a child with no worries. I could not ever remember feeling safe and secure. Resentment and blame would not give me back my childhood. The only answer was to face facts and trust God to give me a double blessing for my former trouble (See Isaiah 61:7). I could not get my childhood back. I would never get to sit on my dad's lap and feel safe, but God could do something even better for me if I would let go of the past and trust Him.

When we stop blaming, God can go to work. He is an expert at fixing what Satan has tried to destroy. He can actually make us better than we ever would have been had we never been hurt at all.

SHAME AND DEPRESSION

Very often a person with a shame-based nature experiences depression. It is impossible for anyone to feel happy if he doesn't like who he is, or if he feels ashamed of himself. There is medicine that may possibly help the symptoms of depression, but no medicine from a drugstore can heal a person from shame. Only the medicine of God's Word can do that. God's Word healed me, and it will do the same thing for you, if you apply it diligently.

Applying God's Word means reading and studying it and stepping out on it. Stepping out on the Word of God means doing what God has instructed us to do in His Word rather than what we think, want, or feel. We follow God's ways, not the world's. We apply His Word to our situations and watch it work as He has promised. Reading the Bible and not applying it to our lives would be like getting medicine from a drugstore and not taking it. We might know about the medicine, but unless we took it, we would never know if it worked or not. We would remain sick even though the medicine we needed was in our possession. Don't just study the Word of God—do it (See James 1:22)!

Although I felt ashamed of my past, I made a decision that I had no reason to be ashamed. I was a child, and I could not have prevented what happened to me. It was not my fault. I had to say that over and over. I had carried a false sense of responsibility for years and felt I was to blame, but I chose to believe God's Word above my feelings. In so doing, I was pressing past guilt and shame.

I had to have my mind renewed (See Romans 12:2). I learned to think about my life and myself in an entirely new way.

You and I can feel something and yet know in our hearts that what we feel is incorrect. Feelings cannot be trusted to tell the truth. They are fickle. They change frequently. When things get difficult in life, I may feel like giving up, yet I know and declare I will not. There are times when I feel lonely and unloved, yet I know the way I feel is incorrect. I recognize my feelings are trying to rule me, and I refuse to give them that privilege. When I realized I had felt ashamed for years, but in reality I had nothing to be ashamed of, that truth started setting me free from a life of emotional pain, insecurity, fear, and guilt.

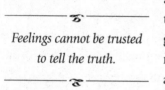

Feelings cannot be trusted to tell the truth.

ADDICTED TO GUILT

I had felt guilty most of my life about one thing or another. I learned that I was a "guilt addict." I just didn't feel *right* if I didn't feel *wrong*. I am sure you have felt that way in the past and may be feeling that way right now.

In my conferences, when I ask for a show of hands of those who are experiencing feelings of guilt, most of the time an overwhelming number of people raise their hands. In the Bible, Satan is called "the accuser of our brethren" (Revelation 12:10). He tries to make us feel guilty and condemned. When we do, it is not God Who is making us feel that way. He wants us to feel loved and forgiven. Guilt depresses us and makes us feel as if we are under a burden. Jesus came to lift us up, to bring the good news that our sins are forgiven and the penalty for them is removed:

> There is therefore now no condemnation to them which are in Christ Jesus, who walk not after the flesh but after the Spirit. (Romans 8:1 KJV)

> Who shall bring any charge against God's elect [when it is] God Who justifies [that is, Who puts us in right relation to Himself? Who shall come forward and accuse or impeach those whom God has chosen? Will God, Who acquits us?]
> Who is there to condemn [us]? Will Christ Jesus (the Messiah), Who died, or rather Who was raised from the dead, Who is at the right hand of God actually pleading as He intercedes for us? (Romans 8:33–34)

Thousands of people are doomed to failure in relationships as well as many other areas simply because they are shame-based, guilt-ridden individuals. Even if they have not done anything wrong, they imagine they have. More than likely they are approval addicts, people who have no peace unless they feel everyone approves of them all the time. They cannot enjoy life because even enjoyment makes them feel guilty.

They look to others to give them what only God can give, which is a sense of self-worth. They are addicted to approval. They need a fresh "fix" of compliments, nods, and glances of approval just to get through the day. They place impossible demands on others because nobody can make them feel good about themselves if they are poisoned inside with guilt and shame.

People who are in relationship with approval addicts feel manipulated instead of loved because the main focus of approval addicts is on feeling good about themselves. Everything centers on them, and soon the other parties in their relationships feel used. These wounded individuals are usually easily offended and touchy. Everyone must walk on eggshells when around them. They cannot be confronted or corrected simply because they already feel so bad about themselves that they cannot handle anyone even mentioning a fault in them or an area about their personality that needs improvement.

Ask yourself how you react to correction or criticism. Try to be honest in your evaluation. Confident people who have validated themselves as valuable can receive correction without anger or a defensive attitude. God says only a fool hates correction (See Proverbs 15:5). Why is that? Because he should be wise enough to want to learn everything he can about himself. Confident people can listen objectively to another point of view; they can pray about what is said and either receive or reject it according to what God places in their hearts.

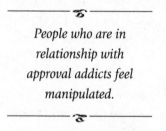

People who are in relationship with approval addicts feel manipulated.

During the years I was filled with shame and guilt, I could not receive even a tiny word of correction from my husband. If he said anything that even remotely suggested he felt I needed to change in any way, I became emotionally upset, angry, and defensive. Dave would repeatedly say, "I am only trying to help you." But I could not get past how I felt when I was given his or anyone else's help. If I asked him whether he liked an outfit I was wearing, I would get defensive if he said no. I could not even allow him to give me his honest opinion. If his opinion did not agree with mine, I felt rejected.

I am grateful that those days are over. Everyone does not have to like what I like in order for me to feel secure. It is absolutely wonderful to be able to approve of ourselves, because we believe God approves of us, even though others do not. It is good to be humble enough to receive correction, yet confident enough not to let the opinions of others control us. Thank God His Holy Spirit is in us, and He will show us what is right for us as individuals.

EXCESSIVE INTROSPECTION

I know all about how shame-based, guilt-ridden people think, feel, and act, because I was one.

One of the problems with shame is that it creates a type of reverse self-centeredness. Shame-based people think about themselves most of the time; even though they are concentrating on what is wrong with them, their mind is still on themselves. They can easily become excessive in self-examination. Although the Bible does teach us to examine ourselves in order to avoid

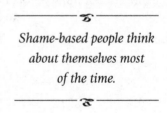

Shame-based people think about themselves most of the time.

judgment from God (See 1 Corinthians 11:28; 2 Corinthians 13:5), we can become excessive in this area.

We are instructed in God's Word to look away from all that will distract us unto Jesus, Who is the Author and Finisher of our faith (See Hebrews 12:2). Stop looking at everything that is wrong with you, and start looking at what is right with Jesus. Learn to identify with Him. Realize He is your Substitute. He took your place and paid the debt you owed. He has opened the prison of guilt, and you can walk out and be free. In order to do so, you will have to press past the pain of guilt and shame you may feel.

The truth makes us free when we apply it to our lives. God's Word is truth (See John 17:17). It tells us that we can live without reproach. We can be presented blameless in His sight:

> Even as [in His love] He chose us [actually picked us out for Himself as His own] in Christ before the foundation of the world, that we should be holy (consecrated and set apart for Him) and blameless in His sight, even above reproach, before Him in love. (Ephesians 1:4)

Be open to anything the Holy Spirit wants to reveal to you about yourself whether that revelation comes through another person, a book you are reading, a sermon you hear, or directly from God Himself. But don't go on a "digging expedition." We don't have to try to "figure ourselves out." The Holy Spirit guides us into all truth (See John 16:13). It is a progressive work, so be patient and let God take the lead.

Enjoy where you are on the way to where you are going.

Ask the Lord to deliver you from every bondage in your life, and let Him choose the timing and method. In the meantime, go ahead and enjoy your life and yourself. Enjoy where you are on the way to where you are going. You may not be where you need to be, but, thank God, you are not where you used to be. You are making progress!

"BUT I FEEL GUILTY"

Establish this as a time for a new beginning. Decide to believe the God of the Bible, not the god of your feelings. Feelings try to be god in our life. They want control. Feelings have been called the believer's number one enemy.[2] Satan works through them to deceive Christians.

The more you renew your mind by studying God's Word, the more your feelings will change. God says that His people are destroyed for a lack of knowledge (See Hosea 4:6).

There is a man I'll call Jake. Jake's father was an angry man. He was an alcoholic and frequently violent when he was drunk. His mother was extremely timid and very fearful of his father. She cowered under whatever he said. Jake's father made him feel guilty all the time. He was like a travel agent for guilt trips. Although Jake sought approval from his father, he could never seem to please him, no matter how hard he tried. Jake spent his teenage and young adult years trying to please people. He had a root of rejection in his life that caused him never to feel he was accepted. He felt lonely and misunderstood. He lived with a vague sense of guilt.

After Jake received Jesus as His Savior at the age of thirty-two and began reading God's Word, he realized that his guilt feelings were a problem. He actually could not remember a time when he did not feel guilty about something. Much of the time he didn't even know anything in particular that he had done wrong; he just felt guilty and condemned.

Jake had no ability to enjoy life. He was a workaholic who hoped to find acceptance and approval through his accomplishments. If he ever did have moments when he felt good about himself, they were immediately following some grand accomplishment for which he was receiving admiration and applause.

Jake also had a false sense of responsibility. When anything went wrong anywhere, he felt it was his responsibility to fix it. Even if it did not directly concern him, he felt he should do something about it. Jake was becoming increasingly depressed by the time he started seeing what his problems actually were.

He was angry about the way his life had turned out. He had bitter feelings toward his father and blamed his mother for not rescuing him.

Our minds may be like some computers that can have a lifetime of wrong information stored in them.

Even after Jake saw the truth in God's Word, he still had all the same feelings. He could read in the Bible that Jesus had delivered him from sin and guilt, but that didn't initially change his feelings.

Our minds may be like some computers that can have a lifetime of wrong information stored in them. It will take time to clean out all the old files and reprogram new information. The Bible says that our minds must be completely renewed (See Romans 12:2). We are like a person who decides she wants to become a lawyer. She realizes at the beginning that it is going to require an investment of many years to learn what she will need to know.

Jake began studying God's Word, and little by little his mind was renewed and he learned to think differently. His fresh new thoughts gradually began to control his old feelings. The feelings did not disappear entirely for quite some time, but he was able to control them. He finally realized that his feelings were reactions to his past life. He began learning to act on God's Word, not react to old memories.

Jake learned the importance of his own self-talk. How we talk to and about ourselves, whether silently or out loud, is vitally important. Get into agreement with God. Say what He says about you. If God says you are forgiven and your guilt has been removed, then you should say the same thing. Don't say how you feel—say what you know!

Jake no longer feels guilty all the time. Once in awhile he still has "a guilt attack," but he can reason with himself and not let his feelings control him. He no longer derives his sense of worth and value from his work. He enjoys his work, but he is able to separate it from who he is as a child of God. He is not addicted to approval. He desires it, but he knows that as long as God approves of him, he already has all he really needs to be successful in life.

Jake has been able to forgive his father. His father still drinks heavily and is still critical most of the time, but Jake no longer receives condemnation from him. He has finally realized that his father is the one with the problem, not him. He no longer feels responsible to keep his father happy. He now knows that his father's problem is inside him; it is not something that can be fixed by someone on the outside. Jake prays for his father and shows him whatever love he will receive. He hopes someday he will be able to lead his father into a personal relationship with Christ. He doesn't blame his mother any longer. He realizes she did the best she could in her condition. She has suffered greatly in her life, and Jake feels compassion for her.

Jake has met a woman and fallen in love with her. Interestingly enough, she has some of the same problems that God has helped Jake overcome. He will be able to help her find restoration through Christ just as he did.

Don't waste yourself on shame and guilt. Use what you have learned to help others. If you have gone through it, you can walk someone else through. What happened to Jake was only made possible through God's Word, Jesus' sacrifice, and the work of the Holy Spirit in his life. The same help is available to every person

―――――― ❧ ――――――
If you have gone through it,
you can walk someone
else through.
―――――― ❧ ――――――

who will receive it. Whatever issues you may be facing in your own life right now, don't let your feelings control you. Compare them to God's Word, and exalt His Word above your feelings. Remember this: You can do what is right even if you feel wrong. Make right choices no matter how you feel, and you will soon be experiencing greater freedom than you have ever known. Making a right choice when you feel wrong equals starving an addiction. If you don't feed it, it will soon lose its strength and have no power over you.

Now that we have addressed addiction to shame and guilt, I want to look at another type of emotion we must conquer in our battle with acceptance.

Pressing Past Anger and Unforgiveness

Do you ever get angry? Of course you do; we all do. God never tells us not to feel anger. He says, "Be ye angry, and sin not" (Ephesians 4:26 KJV). We may feel anger, and that is important, but it is how we process our anger that is most important. It might seem at first that anger has nothing to do with approval addictions, but when we look at the root of excessive anger issues, they almost always find their seed in earlier problems. Anger certainly can be just another facet of our struggle with acceptance. I have found that many people who become frequently angry have a root of insecurity in their life. Those who are easily offended and touchy are insecure. They must be treated good to feel good about themselves. In some ways they expect to be treated badly because down deep inside they feel bad about themselves. However, when they are it angers them because what they feared about themselves has been confirmed, at least in their minds.

The word *anger* is one letter removed from the word *danger*. God's Word tells us not to let the sun go down on our anger (See Ephesians

4:26 KJV). When we stay angry, we give the devil a foothold in our lives (See v. 27). We open a door for him to work. Most of the ground gained by Satan in the Christian's life is gained through bitterness, resentment, and unforgiveness. People who easily fly into a rage always make a bad landing. When our emotions are out of control, so is our life. Anger makes our mouth work faster than our mind. We end up saying and doing things we are sorry for later.

God promises His children a blessed and abundant life, if they obey His commandments. Staying angry and harboring unkind feelings toward others is disobedience. We must realize sustained anger is sin. If we don't look at it for what it is, we may be tempted to hang onto it. William Secker, a seventeenth-century pastor, said, "He that would be angry and not sin, must be angry at nothing but sin." Be angry at the sin of anger, and you won't be tempted to keep it.

In several of the books I have written I have included a chapter on anger. Although as a writer I strive to present fresh material, this is a subject that cannot be ignored. We must be quick to forgive. We must deal properly with the emotion of anger. If we do not, the consequences are devastating.

A wounded person cannot receive emotional healing while remaining angry. God commands us to forgive as freely as He has forgiven us (See Ephesians 4:32). In this life we must be willing to be very generous with forgiveness. It is one thing we usually need to give away, at least to some degree, every day.

"IT ISN'T FAIR"

When we have been mistreated, it seems totally unfair to just forgive those who have hurt us. We feel someone needs to pay for what has happened to us. When we hurt, we want to place blame. We want justice! We need to remember God is just (See Deuteronomy 32:4). His Word promises He will eventually make everything right that is wrong, if we will only trust Him (See Isaiah 61:7–8).

At three o'clock one morning I suddenly awoke and heard what sounded to me like an audible voice that said, "If God is real, then God is just." It was as if God wanted to remind me in a very strong way that I could always count on enjoying His justice in my

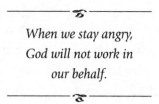

When we stay angry, God will not work in our behalf.

life. This has been comforting to me. The Bible teaches us in Psalm 37 not to fret over evildoers, because they will be dealt with (See vv. 1–2). Verse 8 says, "Cease from anger and forsake wrath; fret not yourself—it tends only to evildoing."

If someone has mistreated us, and we remain angry, we are just as guilty as the one who abused us. God has instructed that individual not to mistreat people, but He has also instructed us not to stay angry. When we stay angry, God will not work in our behalf. God begins where we finish. We are commanded several times in God's Word to forgive those who abuse us or mistreat us, to pray for them and love them, and to wait for God's justice:

> Never return evil for evil or insult for insult (scolding, tongue-lashing, berating), but on the contrary blessing [praying for their welfare, happiness and protection, and truly pitying and loving them];
>
> For know that to this you have been called, that you may yourselves inherit a blessing [from God—that you may obtain a blessing as heirs, bringing welfare and happiness and protection]. (1 Peter 3:9)
>
> But I say to you who are listening now to Me: [in order to heed, make it a practice to] love your enemies, treat well (do good to, act nobly toward) those who detest you and pursue you with hatred,

> Invoke blessings upon and pray for the happiness of those who
> curse you, implore God's blessing (favor) upon those who abuse
> you [who revile, reproach, disparage, and high-handedly misuse
> you]. (Luke 6:27–28)

These instructions are not easy to follow. Obviously it is impossible to do so unless we choose to press past our feelings. Yes, we must *press*. We must make an effort to forgive and to let go of anger. It almost seems unfair of God even to ask us to do such a thing. If you want to know the truth, I actually feel this is one of the most difficult things God asks of us. It is hard, but not impossible. The Lord never requires us to do anything without giving us the ability to do it. We may not want to forgive, but we are able to do so with God's help.

ARE YOU REALLY BEING MISTREATED?

Insecure people often perceive they are being mistreated when in actuality that is not the case at all. I can remember feeling mistreated and angry when Dave did not agree with me about minor issues. His opinion, which he certainly was entitled to have, was merely different than mine but I was so insecure I felt rejected. As they say, "I made mountains out of molehills." I would turn a minor incident into a tragedy because I was so touchy. When I did not get my way, I felt mistreated and became angry. When I was corrected in even a minor way, I responded with anger and felt I was being treated unfairly.

My point is this: it is possible to believe you are being treated unfairly when that is not the case at all. The way I processed people's reactions to me was totally out of balance because of my past abuse. I could not correctly discern when I was genuinely being mistreated compared to when people were simply being honest with me about their own feelings.

The truth is I was very angry because I was very insecure.

SEEKING COMPENSATION

People who have been hurt not only get angry, but often they also seek compensation for injustices done. There is a feeling that some payment is due them for their hurt. God clearly states that vengeance is *His*. He says He will repay our enemies and will compensate us; He actually promises a double blessing for our former trouble (See Romans 12:17–19 and Isaiah 61:7). I finally learned that if someone was truly mistreating me, I did not need to exact compensation. I could trust God to bring whatever justice was necessary, if any was necessary at all.

My father hurt me, and I was so angry that I spent years trying to collect what I thought was due me from people who had nothing to do with my hurt. For instance, God caused me to realize I was trying to collect a debt from my husband, Dave, that he did not owe. My father hurt me, and I didn't trust Dave. My father did not discipline me properly, so I was afraid to let Dave discipline our children. My father misused his authority in my life, so I was rebellious toward Dave's authority.

I know it sounds foolish, but we all have a tendency to do the same thing. We want someone to pay for our pain, and since we frequently cannot collect from the one who hurt us, we lash out at others. They are confused because they have no idea why we respond to them the way we do. God wants us to trust Him to pay us back. He has brought a wonderful reward into my life. He has given me favor and promoted me beyond anything I could ever have imagined, but first I had to "let go and let God be God."

Someone I'll call Janet had this problem. Janet's father did not show her love and affection. When she got married, she expected her husband, John, to pay her back. He, of course, was not required to pay her back for what she missed in her childhood. He did not understand her actions, but then neither did she. She was reacting out of old wounds that still needed to be healed.

Janet required an excessive amount of attention from John. She pressured him to be with her all the time. She was jealous of any friends he had. She never received approval from her father, so she became an approval addict. John had to try to make her feel good about herself at all times. If he failed to tell her she looked nice, or the dinner was great,

> *Let go and let God be God.*

she felt hurt and ignored and she lashed out in anger. John felt controlled and manipulated; although he loved Janet, he was beginning to feel overwhelmed and wondered if he had made a mistake in marrying her. He tried very hard to please her, but nothing ever seemed to be enough; therefore, he felt defeated most of the time.

John had been a happy, easygoing guy when he and Janet got married, but now he was feeling depressed, discouraged, and angry. He dreaded coming home from work at night and did not look forward to weekends. Janet and John needed help!

Sad to say, Janet refused to get help; she blamed everything on John, and ultimately they ended up divorced. This scenario is repeated frequently in our society these days. The divorce rate is higher than ever, and it is partly because people who have been hurt in their past try to make people in their present pay them back for something they had nothing to do with. Because of old wounds they perceive they are being treated wrong when in fact that is not the case at all. They have to learn, just as I had to learn, that if they "feel" hurt it does not necessarily mean someone is really hurting them.

If the people involved in cases of this type are Christians, and they let God do so, He will heal them and bring justice into their lives. If they are not Christians, or if they are Christians but refuse to be obedient to God's instructions, either they will completely ruin their relationship, or at best they will limp along in an unhappy state while their situation gradually gets worse. They will probably begin to see the effects in their physical bodies, and a round of doctor visits will begin. They will end up taking medicine for headaches, body aches, depression, anxiety, sleep disorders, stomach problems, and a long list of other ailments. The medicine may give them some relief, but the root of their problem is stress— stress that has been created by trying to collect compensation for past hurts instead of realizing that their job is to forgive those who hurt them and trust God to pay them back.

Please understand, sometimes medicine is necessary, and I am not dismissing that. But although symptoms are real, they are often stress related. I am only speaking to the underlying causes that many fail to recognize and address spiritually.

STOP WEARING THINGS THAT DON'T FIT

Therefore, as God's chosen people, holy and dearly loved, clothe yourselves with compassion, kindness, humility, gentleness and patience. *Bear with each other and forgive whatever grievances you may have against one another. Forgive as the Lord forgave you.* (Colossians 3:12–13 NIV, emphasis mine)

We are created to receive and give love. If we do anything else, it is like wearing clothes that are too small for us. I absolutely hate to wear a skirt or a pair of pants that are too tight in the waist. All day long I am uncomfortable. Many people are uncomfortable all the time. They feel a burden in their spirit. They have no joy or peace. They may fight feelings of depression regularly. The sad thing is that it is possible to spend one's entire life feeling that way and never face the truth about the root cause.

Hating people is hard work, and it poisons our lives. God tells us in His Word to "put on love" (See Colossians 3:14 NIV). We are to clothe ourselves as representatives of God, Who is love (See Colossians 3:12 and 1 John 4:4). We are instructed to put on behavior that is marked by mercy, tenderhearted pity, kind feelings, gentle ways and patience, which is tireless and long-suffering. We are challenged to be people who have the power to endure whatever comes, with good temper, to readily pardon each other; even as the Lord has freely forgiven us, so we are to forgive one another (See Colossians 3:12–13).

We are created to receive and give love.

God tells us that when we refuse to forgive those who have hurt us, He cannot forgive us our trespasses either (See Matthew 6:15). A refusal to forgive our enemies drives a wedge between us and God. It adversely affects all of our relationships. When we are angry it comes out of us no matter whom we are angry at. A refusal to forgive adversely affects our faith, weighs heavily on our conscience, and prevents true worship. The Bible actually says we cannot say we love God if we don't love our brother and sister in Christ:

If anyone says, I love God, and hates (detests, abominates) his brother [in Christ], he is a liar; for he who does not love his brother, whom he has seen, cannot love God, Whom he has not seen.

And this command (charge, order, injunction) we have from Him; that he who loves God shall love his brother [believer] also. (1 John 4:20–21)

Love is much more than a good feeling about someone. Love is a decision. When we are instructed in God's Word to "put on love," it means that we are to choose to love people. It is something we do on purpose whether we feel like it or not. I don't think I have a choice about whether I will forgive someone who has hurt me or treated me unjustly. I gave up the right to run my own life long ago. I want God's will, so I must do things His way.

Recently there were some very unkind and unfair newspaper articles written about our ministry and family. We agreed to interviews and were told favorable articles would be written based on them. We allowed the photographer who worked for the newspaper to attend our conferences for the purpose of taking pictures. The man must have taken a thousand photographs. But one of the most prominent ones featured in the paper was a large picture of our ushers standing in the back of the room holding stacks of offering buckets. This of course left the impression that we were money-hungry, dishonest ministers who were taking advantage of people.

For four days the front pages of our city newspaper were filled with information about us that was taken out of context and presented in an unbalanced manner. It hurt me deeply. I love the people in my city, and I did not want them to feel they could not trust me. For a while I was embarrassed even to go outside because of what people might be thinking. I was tested on everything I had ever said or written about forgiving our enemies. My confidence level was tested. But I have learned by experience that I could survive even if everyone did not approve of me. God gave me grace to keep on keeping on, but it was hard emotionally.

I so desperately wanted to defend myself against my critics, but God kept telling us to forgive them, pray for them, refuse to talk badly about them, and watch Him work. People in the city who loved us began calling the newspaper and defending us. Actually the articles caused quite a stir at the newspaper office. Many people canceled their subscriptions. One woman called our office and said, "I have never been a contributor to your ministry, but I am canceling my newspaper subscription and will be sending you the money I was paying for it every month from now on."

Making the right choice is worth it in the end.

We waited to see how the articles would affect our ministry. Would people reduce their giving or withdraw it entirely? Would people still attend our conferences? What kind of comments would we get? The outcome was glorious. The ministry grew in every way. Our financial support increased, attendance at our conferences grew, and in general people encouraged us and defended us. We actually felt that the event catapulted us into a new level in our ministry.

It was vitally important for us to obey God during this time and not try to vindicate ourselves. Walking in love is not easy when people are not acting lovely. I really felt the newspaper was very unkind, mean-spirited, and in some cases downright untruthful, but God used the event to promote us. The Bible says in Romans 8:28 NKJV that all things work together for good to those who love God and are called according to His purpose. We kept loving God and doing what we felt God had called us to do. Instead of reacting in anger, we trusted Him to take care of us, and He did.

I wanted to share this example with you because I can still remember the pain I felt when I read those articles. I had just returned from holding an out-of-town conference. I was very tired and not in the mood for a shock. As you read this book, you may be experiencing the pain of being judged and criticized, betrayed, rejected, or disapproved. If so, you may be trying to work through feelings of offense, unforgiveness, bitterness, resentment, and anger. I just want you to know I really do know how you feel, and I know it is not always easy to overcome those feelings.

I also know making the right choice is worth it in the end, so be encouraged by my testimony to press past anger and unforgiveness. I believe if you will do so, you will see God's justice manifested in your life. He will give you double blessings for your former trouble. He will deliver you and promote you, if you keep walking in love.

Do what you know is right, not what you feel like doing!

WHO IS YOUR REAL ENEMY?

Laying blame is a problem, but laying blame in the wrong place is even worse. The Bible says our warfare is with the devil, not with people (See Ephesians 6:12). We desire revenge when people hurt us, but if the devil is really the one behind all of our pain, how can we get him back?

The Bible says we overcome evil with good (See Romans 12:21). Satan is evil, and the way to get back at him is to aggressively be good to everyone we meet, including our enemies. It is not natural to pray for one's enemies or to bless them. It is not the response the devil expects or hopes for. When we do become angry and bitter, we play right into his hands. We open a door for him to walk through and allow him to gain access to many areas of our lives through an unforgiving attitude. Our joy is adversely affected, as is our health, our peace, our prayer life, our sleep habits, et cetera. Unity and agreement produce power, so it stands to reason that disagreement and disunity produce powerlessness.

KEEP THE STRIFE OUT

I believe strife is initiated by demonic spirits sent out by Satan. Their job is to prevent joy, peace, progress, and prosperity. They are sent to destroy businesses, churches, ministries, marriages, and all other such institutions and relationships.

We are instructed by God to keep strife out of our lives (See Philippians 2:3 KJV). That is impossible to do unless we are willing to forgive freely and frequently. The ability to forgive requires an attitude of humility. We must realize we also need forgiveness—from God and from others—on a regular basis.

Contention comes only by a prideful attitude. It cannot come any other way. Where there is bickering and arguing, there is a haughty spirit that views itself as better than others (See James 3:14–16). The Bible says in Romans 2:1 that we judge others for the same things we do. We make excuses for our wrong actions. We give ourselves mercy, but are not willing to do the same for others. God will hold us accountable for this type of attitude. He requires us to forgive and press past anger.

The ability to forgive requires an attitude of humility.

Paul told the church located at Phillipi that he would be made happy if they would live in harmony:

Fill up and complete my joy by living in harmony and being of the same mind and one in purpose, having the same love, being in full accord and of one harmonious mind and intention. (Philippians 2:2)

Paul was aware of God's wonderful plan for His children. He wanted everyone to receive the best God had for them, and he knew that would be impossible if they did not live in harmony. We are repeatedly taught in Scripture to live in peace. In the Bible, Jesus Himself is called the "Prince of Peace"(Isaiah 9:6).

God has clearly instructed Dave and me that we must keep strife out of our life and ministry if we want to be successful at what He has called us to do. In order to do so, we must be generous with forgiveness. We must refuse to let bitterness take root in our hearts (See Hebrews 12:15). We cannot allow ourselves to be offended or remain angry. This means we cannot follow our feelings; we must press past feelings and do what God asks us to do.

Sometimes God asks us to simply let something go and not even mention it; at other times He requires us to confront and communicate openly about situations. Communication often clears up confusion and brings balance to situations that cause conflict. When people don't like to confront it is usually because they don't want anyone to be displeased with them or think badly of them. If a person has an addiction to approval they normally will not confront issues head on. This lack of confrontation opens the door for greater misunderstanding and strife.

Resist the temptation to let anger take root in your heart.

There are also times when we just need to be patient and pray about a situation. Discerning how to handle each situation is a real key. A Chinese proverb says, "If you are patient in one moment of anger, you will escape a hundred days of sorrow." The person who can anger you has power over you. Each time you allow yourself to remain angry, you poison your own system. The Bible clearly states that the anger of man does not promote the righteousness that God desires (See James 1:20).

Strive to stay out of strife. Make an effort to live in peace with everyone (See Romans 12:18). Resist the temptation to let anger take root in your heart. I have found the more quickly I forgive, the less likely I am to have a real problem. The Bible teaches us to resist the devil at his onset (See 1 Peter 5:8–9). Don't wait too long to do what you know God wants you to do. The longer you wait, the harder it will be to obey.

When young David looked at the giant, Goliath, he ran quickly toward the battle line (See 1 Samuel 17:48). I think David knew that if he thought about Goliath too long, he might run away. He took action to obey God right away, and we need to always do the same. When God prompts us to take some action, His grace is present to enable us. When we do things in our own timing, we often have to do them in our own strength.

FOUR STEPS TO VICTORY

You may choose to forgive and yet find your feelings toward the person who hurt you are still quite unforgiving. Forgiveness is a choice you make and you must earnestly work toward that goal.

But understand it may take time. And that is okay. If we do what we can do, God will do what we cannot do. We cannot make wrong feelings go away any more than we can make right ones come, but God can and will. If we will simply do what Scripture instructs us to do, we will be able to work through the process of forgiveness. The first thing we must do is to forgive those who have hurt us. The second thing is to pray for them as God has told us to do. Another thing God tells us to do is to bless our enemies, so that is the third thing. To bless someone means to speak well of them and want good things for them. Refuse to talk unkindly about those who hurt you. Don't keep talking about what your enemies did that hurt you. It only keeps the pain stirred up in you.

I also believe we can and should bless our enemies in practical ways when it is appropriate. Once God led me to send gift certificates to someone who had been talking unkindly about me. The moment I did, I felt a release from the wound, and joy filled my soul. I did not send that person a gift because I thought that individual deserved one. I did it because God blesses those who do not deserve it, and I wanted to be like Him.

The fourth thing we must do is wait: "And let us not be weary in well doing: for in due season we shall reap, if we faint not" (Galatians 6:9 KJV). Don't give up. Keep doing what is right, and wait on God to change your feelings.

I have applied these four principles in my life and have seen victory over adverse feelings every time.

LEARNING A NEW RESPONSE

Our problems are not really what defeat us; it is our angry and vengeful response to them. Responding to offense with forgiveness

CHAPTER

Pressing Past a "People-Pleaser" Attitude

We are to be God-pleasers, not self-pleasers or people-pleasers. If we are approval addicts, we are probably also people-pleasers. We usually discover in our experience that if we don't please people, they don't approve of us; therefore, if we have an out-of-balance need for approval, we have no choice but to be people-pleasers.

Wanting to be pleasing and be acceptable is a natural trait. We might even say it is godly. God wants us to be good to people and strive to accommodate them. Scripture teaches us to make it a practice to please our neighbor:

Let each one of us make it a practice to please (make happy) his neighbor for his good and for his true welfare, to edify him [to strengthen him and build him up spiritually].

For Christ did not please Himself [gave no thought to His own interests]. (Romans 15:2–3)

The apostle Paul said in Galatians that he did not seek popularity with man, yet in 1 Corinthians he stated that he tried to please people and accommodate himself to their opinions and desires in order that they might be saved:

Now am I trying to win the favor of men, or of God? Do I seek to please men? If I were still seeking popularity with men, I should not be a bond servant of Christ (the Messiah). (Galatians 1:10)

Just as I myself strive to please [to accommodate myself to the opinions, desires, and interests of others, adapting myself to] all men in everything I do, not aiming at or considering my own profit and advantage, but that of the many in order that they may be saved. (1 Corinthians 10:33)

When we consider these two verses of Scripture, they almost seem to contradict one another, yet they don't if we understand the heart behind them.

Paul wanted to please people. He wanted to maintain good relationships with people, especially for the purpose of leading them to accept Jesus as their Savior. He also wanted to please God and fulfill the call on his life. Paul knew how to maintain balance in this area. He tried to please people, as long as pleasing them did not cause him to displease the Lord. The Bible says in Acts 5:29, "We must obey God rather than men."

> *Pleasing people is good, but it is not good to become people-pleasers.*

Pleasing people is good, but it is not good to become people-pleasers. I would define people-pleasers as those who try to please people even if they have to compromise their conscience to do so. People-pleasers are those who need approval so desperately that they allow themselves to be controlled, manipulated, and used by others. They are not led by the Holy Spirit, as Scripture instructs us to be (See Romans 8:14).

People-pleasers are fear-based individuals. They fear rejection, judgment, what people think and say, and especially anger or disapproval.

CHECK YOUR MOTIVES

Our reason or motive for doing the things we do is very important. God wants us to have pure hearts. He wants us to do what we do because we believe He is leading us to do it or because it is the right thing to do. God wants us to be motivated by love. We should do what we do for the love of God and man. If we are motivated by fear, it does not please God.

We should regularly take some time and ask ourselves why we are doing the things we do. It is not what we do that impresses God; it is the "why" behind what we do that He is concerned with.

God instructs us in His Word not to do good deeds to be seen of men. We are not to do things to be recognized and honored. When we pray, we are not to do it to be seen of men or to try and impress God by heaping up phrases and repeating them over and over. God is not impressed with the length and eloquence of our prayers. He is searching for sincerity and fervency. Any work of ours that is impure will be burned up on Judgment Day. We lose our reward for any work that is done with impure motives (See Matthew 6:1–7 and 1 Corinthians 3:13–15).

If we do things for people, and our motives are impure, we are out of God's will. Not every work that appears to be good is good. A work is good only if it is done in the will of God. Two people can do the same "good deed," and yet God may not consider it good for both of them. One of the two may be in the will of God, and the other may be out of the will of God, depending on their motives for their actions.

I strive to do what I do with right motives. If I am asked to attend a function, and I really don't feel led by God to go, or if I know my schedule cannot accommodate it without it becoming stressful, I don't go! When people want to hear yes, and you tell them no, they never like it. But those who are truly your friends will give you the freedom to make your own decisions. They will respect the decisions you make. They will not pressure you or try to make you feel guilty for not pleasing them. Your true friends are not those who are merely using you for their own benefit or those who always become angry when you don't do what they want you to do.

It is our responsibility to stand up to people who try to control us. If we don't, we are just as guilty as they are. If people try to control us, they are acting against God's will, but if we do not confront them, we are also acting against God's will.

> *It is our responsibility to stand up to people who try to control us.*

We must not blame others if we are fearful and timid. It is offensive to God when we fear people more than we fear Him. We should not fear God in a wrong way, but we should have a respectful fear of Him, knowing that He means what He says. Since God has told us in His Word that we are not to be people-pleasers, we should take that commandment seriously and not allow an out of balance people-pleasing attitude in our lives.

Live to please God, and you will never be an approval addict.

What you think of yourself is more important than what others think of you. You cannot feel good about yourself if you know what you are doing does not have God's approval on it. It is not good if you say yes and yet disrespect yourself because you cannot say no.

According to Romans 8:14, all who are led by the Spirit of God are the sons of God. Mature Christians are led by God's Spirit, not by other people. They have learned to trust their own heart. They follow peace, not people (See Hebrews 12:14 KJV).

GO WITH GOD

The Bible teaches us in John 12:42–43 that many of the leading men believed in Jesus but would not confess it for fear that if they did, they would be expelled from the synagogue. "They loved the approval and the praise and the glory that come from men [instead of and] more than the glory that comes from God" (v. 43).

In this example we see that some people were hindered from a relationship with Jesus because they were addicted to approval. Although they wanted a relationship with the Lord, they loved the approval of man more. That is sad, but it happens all the time.

I know a woman who had deep emotional problems. She attended a Bible study group where she received the infilling of the Holy Spirit. She was overwhelmed with joy. God had touched her, and she knew it. When she told her brothers and sisters, they told her she was crazy. They told her she needed to be careful of "emotional experiences." They told her that what she had experienced could have been from the devil and not from God at all. They frightened her, and because she was afraid of what people would think of her, she did not pursue her newfound relationship with the Lord. The woman was a Christian and attended church, so she simply kept quiet and continued following the prescribed guidelines of her particular religious denomination, which did not support such "experiences" with God. She also went back to being depressed and neurotic. God tried to help her, but she loved the approval of people more than His approval.

I am not advocating seeking spiritual experiences, but if God visits us, and we do experience Him, it is not to be denied. I would imagine that the apostle Paul had quite an experience on the Damascus road as Jesus spoke to him, and His power knocked Paul to the ground (See Acts 9:1–20). I have found that people have a ten-dency to rule out anything they have not personally experienced. The Bible teaches us that there will be people who hold a form of religion but are strangers to the power of it (See 2 Timothy 3:5). I have found that the doctrines of man can steal the power of God.

Follow God, not people!

Follow God, not people! The people mentioned in John 12 knew that Jesus was real. They believed in Him, but the love of approval would not permit them to have a true relationship with Him. I wonder how their lives turned out. What did they miss because they said yes to people and no to God? I wonder how many of them were never mentioned in the Bible again. I wonder if they faded into oblivion and never fulfilled their destiny because they loved the approval of men more than the approval of God. How many of them spent their lives disrespecting themselves because they were people-pleasers?

Not everyone is going to like us. I recently read somewhere that statistically 2 percent of the population won't like us, and there is nothing we can do about it but accept it and go on about our business. If we live our lives worrying about what other people think, we will never take risks or stretch ourselves into new realms. We will give up our dreams.

Satan is a dream thief, and he works through people who are selfish enough to steal our dreams in order to have theirs. The people close to you may not understand or agree with how you want to live your life. If you care too much, one day you will wake up and realize you have never really lived at all, you have just been manipulated and used by people who didn't really care about you after all.

Everyone is entitled to his opinion, and the information and feedback we receive from others can be valuable. We must not automatically reject what others think, but we must not let it control us either. We must remember that what people say is just their opinion, not necessarily fact. What they think may be right for them and wrong for us.

You are an individual, with individual rights. Don't let anyone steal from you what Jesus died to give you—which is the freedom to follow the leading of the Holy Spirit for you as an individual.

DUTY OR DESIRE

In the life of people-pleasers, the driving force is duty, not desire. They do many things out of a feeling of obligation. They have trouble saying no when asked to do something. If we do something good, but we do it with resentment, feeling used and pressured, we have no joy and no reward.

Remember, unless we do what we do for right reasons, we lose our reward. We do have biblical duties. For example, Scripture tells us it is our duty to care for our families (See 1 Timothy 5:8). If we have elderly parents or grandparents, it is our duty to provide for them. It is a duty we must perform whether we feel like it or not. You may have dependent elderly parents who never really took proper care of you. They may have even abused you. Is it really your duty to take care of them now? Yes, it is. If you cannot do it for them, do it for God, and do it with a good attitude. It is your duty.

We do have biblical duties, but on the other hand we should not allow the "shoulds" and "oughts" of life to control us. There is a big difference in doing our duty before God and being duty bound to people.

For example, don't go in debt every Christmas just because you feel you should buy gifts for relatives you don't even like. Are you buying gifts for people because you are afraid of what they may think if you don't? Or are you buying them because of your need to have them appreciate you? You may even buy gifts for people so they will give you one back. If so, your motives are wrong. It is not God's will that you go in debt to buy gifts. Be bold enough to tell the truth.

YOU HAVE LEGITIMATE NEEDS YOURSELF

People-pleasers quickly and regularly set aside their own legitimate needs. Denying them eventually builds into an explosive situation. Constantly trying to please others is draining, which is why many people-pleasers feel anxious, worried, unhappy, and tired much of the time. They resent the fact that other people don't do much for them, but they often deny the fact that they have legitimate needs.

People-pleasers may think if they ask for help, they may make others feel obligated. Although they do most of what they do out of a sense of obligation, they don't want others to feel that way toward them. They believe people would not want to do anything for them anyway. Most people-pleasers feel that way because they have a poor self-image. They don't value themselves, so they think nobody else values them either.

It is likely most people-pleasers were raised in homes in which their needs and feelings were not valued, respected, or considered important. As children, they were expected to respond to or take care of other

> *People-pleasers quickly and regularly set aside their own legitimate needs.*

people's needs. The focus of most people-pleasers is primarily toward others and away from themselves. Sometimes they don't even know what they feel or think or even what they want for themselves. They have become so good at denying their own needs, they don't even ask themselves if they have any.

Someone I'll call Patty was raised in a dysfunctional home. Patty's father was an alcoholic and verbally abusive. As a result, she learned to totally disregard her needs and to spend her time taking care of others. She developed a martyr complex. She did things for people, but resented doing it. Patty felt taken advantage of, but would not accept anything for herself even when it was offered. She did not feel she was worth anything, so she would not receive anything.

Patty lived with tremendous stress, most of which she placed on herself because of the way she had been raised. She was diagnosed with severe arthritis, which was causing her tremendous pain. Her emotional and physical pain joined together was more than she could handle. She became very depressed.

Patty began going to a counselor who asked her what she wanted out of life. She could not tell him because she had never even thought about what *she* wanted. She had to do a lot of soul searching and learn that having needs and desires was not wrong. She had been so accustomed to not getting anything she wanted in life that she simply did not bother wanting anything at all. She was afraid to desire anything because she felt she had no right to do so. She felt worthless and devalued.

We all have needs, especially emotional needs.

It was very refreshing to watch Patty begin to learn that it was acceptable to have legitimate needs and to expect people to meet them. She began to have hopes and dreams for her life, and it gave her something to look forward to. She is well on the road to release from her people-pleasing addiction.

We all have needs, especially emotional needs. Denying them eventually builds into explosive situations. What do we need emotionally? We need love, encouragement, and companionship—someone to connect to and confide in. We need acceptance, approval, and enjoyment.

GOD WANTS YOU TO ENJOY YOURSELF

When I was growing up, I did not enjoy myself. I was never really allowed to act like a child. I can remember getting into trouble and being corrected for playing. Our house was not enjoyable. It was filled with fear.

As an adult Christian, I began to realize I felt guilty if I attempted to enjoy myself. I felt safe if I was working, but enjoyment was something I denied myself. I did not feel it was a legitimate need for me. I resented other people who were not working as long and hard as I was. My husband really enjoyed his life, and it made me angry. I felt that he could accomplish so much more in life if he would just be more serious.

I realize now that I was not angry because Dave enjoyed his life; I was angry because I did not enjoy mine. But I was the only one who could do anything about it. It was foolish of me to resent Dave and other people, because the enjoyment they had in life was also available to me for the taking.

I did not like myself. Deep down inside I believed I was no good, and I punished myself for being bad by refusing to enjoy anything. After all, bad people don't deserve to enjoy life!

The Holy Spirit worked with me a long time before I finally understood that God wanted me to enjoy my life. Jesus actually said, "I came that you might have and enjoy your life" (See John 10:10). We need enjoyment. Without it, life is unbalanced, and a door is opened for Satan to devour us (See 1 Peter 5:8). The joy of the Lord is our strength (See Nehemiah 8:10). There is a time to work and a time to play, a time to cry and a time to laugh (See Ecclesiastes 3:1–8).

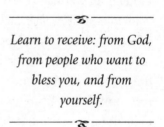

Learn to receive: from God, from people who want to bless you, and from yourself.

Make sure you are not denying your legitimate needs. It is good to help others; as Christians, it is our call. But, it is not wrong to do things for ourselves. Be sure you take time for yourself. Take time to do things you enjoy.

Learn to receive: from God, from people who want to bless you, and from yourself. The only persons you should not receive from are the devil and people being used by him. If someone gives you a compliment, graciously accept it. If someone belittles you, reject it. If someone shows you love and kindness, receive it. If someone rejects you, do what Jesus told His disciples to do: shake it off and go on!

Be determined to enjoy your life. You only go around once, so be sure you enjoy the ride.

"I FEEL BAD WHEN I DON'T PLEASE PEOPLE"

Do you feel bad when you don't please people? Many years ago I began to realize that the reason I tried so hard to please people was to benefit me rather than them. If I could please them, then *I* felt good. I don't think I really cared all that much about how they felt, it was *me* I was concerned about. Did it ever occur to you that people-pleasing can very well be a manifestation of selfishness rather than sacrifice?

People-pleasers feel awful when their decisions do not please others. They assume responsibility for other people's emotional reactions. In my former life, if I thought someone was angry, unhappy, or disappointed, it made me uncomfortable. I could not feel comfortable again until I thought I had done whatever needed to be done to make that person happy again.

I did not realize that as long as I was following God's will for my life, other people's responses were not my responsibility. It may not always be possible to do what other people want, but a spiritually mature person learns to deal with disappointment and keep a good attitude. If you are doing what you believe God has told you to do, and others are not pleased with you, it is not your fault; it is theirs.

When I was growing up, my father was angry most of the time. I spent most of my time playing the peacemaker in the home. I constantly tried to keep him happy. I was afraid of his anger.

When I became an adult, I continued this practice, except I did it with everybody. Anytime I was with anyone who seemed unhappy, I always felt it was probably my fault; and even if it wasn't my fault, I felt I needed to fix it. I did whatever I thought would please people just so they would stay happy, not realizing that their personal happiness was their responsibility, not mine.

If my husband corrected our children, and they became angry, Dave said it was their problem. He knew he needed to correct them, and how they responded was between them and God. But if I corrected them, and it made them angry, I tried to make them happy again as soon as I had corrected them. In the process, I negated any correction I tried to give. I comforted them before they could feel the effects of being corrected.

When I corrected one of our children or even later in life one of our employees, I spent excessive amounts of time explaining why I was doing what I was doing. I knew I needed to bring the correction, but I did not want anyone to be angry; therefore, I tried to talk people into liking the fact that I was correcting them. What could have taken five minutes or less would often require forty-five minutes or more because of all my efforts to make sure everyone was happy with the way I corrected them.

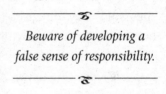

Beware of developing a false sense of responsibility.

My husband tried to tell me what I was doing, but I was so deceived in this area that I just could not see it until God Himself revealed it to me.

I told myself that I did not want people to be hurt, confused, or upset. In reality I did not want anyone to be angry with *me*. I did not want anyone to think badly of *me*. It was really all about *me*.

If you are not able to give people what they want, and they become unhappy, it is not your fault. Beware of developing a false sense of responsibility. You have enough legitimate responsibilities in life without taking on illegitimate ones.

If you tell your children no about something because you feel what they want would not be good for them, it is not your responsibility to make them enjoy hearing no. That is something they will hopefully grow into as they mature; but some people never like hearing no, no matter how old they are. We all need to hear no once in a while; if we don't, we will never be happy with anything other than getting everything our own way.

I would venture to say that if you never tell your children no, then you are not showing proper love. *Be the parent!* You may want to be friends with your children, just as I did, but you cannot always be both parent and friend at the same time.

One time a woman who worked for me came to me and asked if she could talk to me as a friend. I said yes. She began telling me how unhappy she was with her wages as well as some other issues concerning her job. She could not understand why her conversation was upsetting to me. After all, she was just talking to me as a friend! I finally told her that although I wanted to be her friend, I could not be her boss and her friend at the same time in this particular situation. She might not have wanted to hear me saying no to her, but I knew I had to say it.

If you are in authority—and I would venture to say that everyone has authority over something even if it is only the cat or the dog—you must realize that you can rarely make decisions that please everyone all the time. If you are addicted to approval, you will make a poor authority figure.

LIVING WITHIN LIMITS

People-pleasers do not live within limits or margins. In their efforts to please people, they push themselves beyond reasonable boundaries. Let's face it—people often expect us to do things we either should not do or cannot do.

It is painful being a people-pleaser. Some people-pleasers rarely focus on themselves in a proper manner. When they do take a moment for themselves, they feel selfish, indulgent, and guilty, which is why they are often on the go, rushing to get things done, striving to keep everyone happy. Because they stay so busy doing for others, they usually work harder than most people. Because they accomplish so much and are so easy to get along with, they are often the first to be asked to do things. As a result, they are vulnerable to being taken advantage of because they have difficulty saying no. They usually don't even consider that saying no is an option for them. They just assume that they should do whatever anyone asks them to do, no matter how unreasonable it is. When they do venture out and say no to a request, they often change that no to a yes if people act angry or displeased.

People-pleasers will push beyond the bounds of reason, if they think it means everyone will be happy with them. Most people will take advantage of us if we let them. It is just human nature to do so. Don't depend on others to treat you fairly and honestly. You must take the responsibility not to let them take advantage of you.

Often we become bitter and resentful toward those who do take advantage of us, not realizing that we are just as guilty as they are, if not more so. It is my responsibility to manage my life under the direction of the Holy Spirit. It is impossible for others to keep taking advantage of me unless I allow it. They may do it once or twice before I realize what is going on, but once I become aware of what is happening, I become responsible for stopping it.

I once had an employer who took advantage of me. He required me to work so many hours that it kept me from spending proper time with my family. I was worn out and never had time for myself. He never showed appreciation and no matter what I did he always expected something more. If I even mildly indicated that I might not be able to comply with one of his requests his anger would start to surface and I would cave in and agree to do what he had asked of me.

> *It is impossible for others to keep taking advantage of me unless I allow it.*

As the years went by I resented his control more and more. I felt he should be caring enough to realize that he was requiring too much of me. I wanted him to see that my life was out of balance and care enough about me to say, "Take some time off, you certainly deserve it."

As I was praying about the situation one day and moaning to God about how unfair it was, He said, "What your boss is doing is wrong, but you not confronting him is just as wrong." This was hard for me to hear. Like most people I wanted to blame someone else for my lack of courage. Had I not been a people-pleaser and had I not been afraid I would have saved myself about five years of being so stressed that it eventually made me very sick. My boss wasn't my problem; I was my problem. As I said earlier, many people will take advantage of us if we allow it. I allowed him to take advantage.

It is important to realize that God has given you authority first and foremost over your own life. If you don't accept and exercise that authority, you may spend your life blaming others for things you should be doing something about. You should make your own decisions according to what you believe God's will is for you. On

Judgment Day God will not ask anyone else to give an account of your life; He will ask only you (See Matthew 12:36 and 1 Peter 4:5)!

What if Jesus asks you on Judgment Day why you never got around to fulfilling His call on your life? Are you going to tell Him people took advantage of you and you just couldn't do anything about it? Are you going to tell Him you were so busy pleasing people you just never got around to pleasing Him? If you do offer those types of excuses, do you really believe they will be acceptable?

ESTABLISH BOUNDARIES

Just as a person puts up a fence around his property to keep intruders out, so you must establish limits and margins—invisible lines you draw in your life to protect yourself from being used and abused. If you had a privacy fence around your yard, and on a sunny afternoon you looked out into your yard and saw your neighbors sunbathing while their children played without permission, what would you do? You certainly would not just say, "Oh my, I do wish those neighbors would leave me alone." You would probably be very forceful in letting them know that your yard is off limits to them for such activities without your permission.

You need to be just as forceful in letting people know you expect them to respect the limits and margins you have erected around your personal life.

If you don't want friends showing up at your house without calling ahead of time and getting your approval, don't just let them do it and then resent them for it. Enforce your guideline even if you end up losing your friends.

A friend I'll call Henry never seemed to have any money with him when he and James went out to eat or to a movie. Actually

Henry always managed to leave his wallet at home. James always ended up paying the bill with a promise from Henry to pay him back. James did not mind the first couple of times this occurred, but he soon realized that it happened too often to be an accident. And even if it was just a bad habit, Henry needed to break it. James also soon realized that although Henry promised to pay the money back, he always forgot that, too.

Enforce your guideline even if you end up losing your friends.

Resentment became so strong in James's heart that he realized he needed to confront Henry. In a loving way James told Henry, "I really need you to pay your own way and stop forgetting your money." He said, "I cannot afford to pay for both of us, and not only that, I feel taken advantage of." Henry became very angry, telling James he was selfish and should know that eventually he would pay him back. James began to feel guilty, thinking perhaps he was a bad friend, so he apologized.

Henry paid his own way the next three or four times they went out, but soon fell back into the same old pattern. Not only did he forget his money regularly, but he also seemed to be more and more disrespectful in his attitude toward James. Obviously Henry was wrong in being dishonest and taking advantage of James. He was wrong in treating him disrespectfully. But James was just as guilty for letting him do it.

Eventually their friendship completely fell apart, and James had to receive counseling at church to get over the bitterness he felt toward Henry. Henry went on to do the same thing to anyone who let him. He never respected those who did allow him to take advantage of them. The few who stood up to him and made him respect their rights were the only ones he respected.

Always remember that if you let others take advantage of you, it is your fault, not theirs.

DELEGATE OR FALL APART

Although it is difficult for people-pleasers to do, it is wise to set proper limits and margins. It is a sign of strength, not weakness. Asking for help is a good thing to do also. God has placed certain people in each of our lives to help us. If we do not receive their help, we become frustrated and overworked, and they feel unfulfilled because they are not using their gifts. Remember that God has not called you to do everything for everybody in every situation. You cannot be all things to all people all the time. You have legitimate needs. It is not wrong to need help and ask for it. However, it is wrong to need help and be too proud to ask for it.

In Exodus 18:12–27, we see that Moses was a man with many responsibilities. The people looked to him for everything, and he tried to meet all their needs. His father-in-law saw what Moses was doing and said to him, "What is this that you do for the people? Why do you sit alone, and all the people stand around you from morning till evening?" (v. 14). Moses proceeded to tell his father-in-law how all the people came to him with their questions. They wanted him to sit as judge between them and their neighbors whenever a problem existed between them. The people wanted Moses to meet their needs, and he wanted to please them.

It may appear that our sacrifices are good. We may feel proud of ourselves because of our "good" works, and yet they are not good at all. Moses' father-in-law told him the thing he was doing was not good. He told Moses that he would wear out both himself and the people. How could the people get worn out from doing nothing? Because doing nothing can actually be more tiring than doing something. If God has called and equipped you to do something, and someone else is doing it for you all the time, you will feel frustrated. If God has called someone else to help you and you won't allow them to help, he or she will feel unfulfilled and frustrated, too. God has created us to be interdependent on one another. We need each other!

———— ✺ ————

We need each other!

———— ✺ ————

Moses' father-in-law suggested that Moses delegate some of his authority to others. He said Moses should let them make the less important decisions and Moses should deal only with the hard cases. Moses did what his father-in-law suggested, and it enabled him to endure the strain of his task. And the others had the benefit of a sense of accomplishment for the decisions they made on their own.

Many people either complain all the time about what they are expected to do or they end up falling apart emotionally and physically because they won't let anyone help them do anything. They don't think anyone is as qualified for the job as they are. It is easy to think you are more important than you actually are. Learn to delegate. Let as many people help you as possible. If you do, you will last a lot longer and enjoy yourself a lot more.

"I FEEL I SHOULD BE ABLE TO DO MORE"

Comparing ourselves with other people often causes us to put a lot of unnecessary pressure on ourselves. If we observe in our comparison that they can do more things than we can, or that their endurance is greater than ours, we often feel we should be able to do more. Because we feel guilty, we may push ourselves beyond our reasonable limits and end up sick and unhappy.

We are all different, and we all have different limits. Know yourself, and don't feel bad if you cannot do what someone else can do. Even our God-given temperaments help determine what our limits in life will be in various areas.

I know someone—I'll call her Pat—who was married and had three children. She was a full-time mother and homemaker, but unless she had help cleaning her home once a week she struggled to get everything done and remain peaceful.

Pat had a friend named Mary who was also married and had five children. Mary worked outside the home two days a week and did all her own housework, cooking, and laundry with

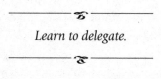

Learn to delegate.

no outside help. Actually it seemed Mary was more peaceful and less temperamental than Pat, even though she had more to do.

Pat felt very bad about herself because she just could not seem to get everything done without help. In her thoughts and conversations, she constantly compared herself to Mary. She felt she should be more like her.

Mary's temperament was easygoing, the "cast your care" type. Her attitude was, "If the work doesn't get done today, it will get done tomorrow." Pat, on the other hand, was very melancholy, a borderline perfectionist who wasn't comfortable unless everything was in order.

We really cannot control what temperament we are born with; that is God's choice. We can work with the Holy Spirit to achieve balance, but basically we are what we are. I will always be a type-A, strong-willed, leadership-type person. In fact, most of the time I am type A+. Dave will always be more easygoing than I am, but that does not mean I have to strive to be like him. I may learn some things from his example, but I still have to be the basic person God created me to be.

Pat put herself under so much pressure that she became difficult to get along with. She carried a burden of guilt most of the time, and it started affecting her mood and her health. She finally got help through a book she read that helped her understand we are all different, and that is perfectly acceptable.

Some people do things faster than others, but the slower person may do them more neatly. Each of us must do what we are comfortable with. It was not wrong for Pat to need a housekeeper once a week and Mary not need one. I am sure that in some other area, Mary had some needs that Pat did not have.

Just be yourself, and don't pressure yourself to perform exactly the way others do.

> *Don't pressure yourself to perform exactly the way others do.*

Pat felt she should be able to do more because she saw Mary do more, but the fact was that she could not do more and maintain her composure. That was not a weakness in her; it was just the way she was put together by God. She did not need to be able to do what Mary did in order to approve of herself. She felt Mary was judging her, when in reality she was judging herself and Mary hadn't thought anything about it.

Concern about what people may be thinking of us often controls us. We are excessively concerned about what people are saying about us. We assume people are thinking certain critical things when the truth is they were not thinking about us at all!

When we seek favor and acceptance from our critics, we lose confidence or stray from the path of healthy choices. Stand up to your critics or you will end up being controlled. The apostle Paul had plenty of critics, but he did not let their opinions control him; neither did Jesus.

> *God has not given and never will give someone else the job of running your life.*

Do the best you can, be the best "you" that you can be, and do not feel you should be able to do more just because someone else does more. And remember a strong confidence in God and your own ability to hear from God and being led by the Spirit are the antidote. God has not given and never will give someone else the job of running your life.

DISHONESTY IS A SYMPTOM OF PEOPLE-PLEASING

Let our lives lovingly express truth [in all things, speaking truly, dealing truly, living truly]. (Ephesians 4:15)

People-pleasing behavior can be quite dishonest. The Bible says we are to be truthful in all things; we are to speak the truth, love the truth, and walk in the truth. But approval addicts often tell lies because they fear people won't accept the truth. They say yes with their mouth while their heart is screaming no. They may not want to do something, but they act as if they do for fear of displeasing someone. If they ever do say no, they usually make an excuse for why they cannot do what is being asked of them. They won't tell the truth, which may be simply that they just plain don't want to do what they are being asked to do. They may not feel it is the right thing for them to do.

Sometimes we don't feel peaceful about a certain thing, and we don't have any idea why. The Scriptures teach us to follow after peace; it is one of the ways God leads us. We should be able to say to people, "I don't have peace about making that commitment right now," and they should graciously receive that answer, but it rarely happens.

I was talking with a fellow minister recently. The man is quite humorous and very bold. He related how another minister had called him with a request for him to appear on his television show. My friend told the man that he could not do so because he had a prior commitment. The man responded that his prior commitment could not possibly be as important as coming on his television show and suggested that he break the previous commitment, to which my friend responded, "I don't want to."

His truthful response ended the conversation immediately. If we would just be bold enough to speak the truth, we could save ourselves a lot of time and trouble.

We don't want to be rude, but neither do we want to be liars. Most people-pleasers are not honest about their desires, feelings, and thoughts. They tell people what they want to hear, not what they need to hear. A healthy relationship demands honesty. Some people may not want to hear truth, but that does not relieve us of the responsibility to speak the truth.

AN EXAMPLE FROM THE LIFE OF KING SAUL

Saul was anointed to be king of Israel. He had an opportunity to enjoy a great and glorious future, but he had some weaknesses in his character that proved to be his undoing (See 1 Samuel 9–31).

Saul was a people-pleaser. He loved the approval of people so much that he disobeyed God's instructions in order to get it. God instructed Saul to wait until the prophet Samuel arrived to offer up the evening sacrifice. When Samuel didn't arrive at the time Saul and the people expected he would, the people became restless and impatient. Although Saul knew in his heart that he was being disobedient, he went ahead and offered the sacrifice that he had been forbidden to offer. Later when Samuel arrived, he asked Saul why he had done so. Saul's reply was, "Because I saw that the people were scattering from me" (1 Samuel 13:11). In response, Samuel told Saul, "You have done foolishly! . . . Now your kingdom shall not continue" (vv. 13–14). Saul was so addicted to approval that he lost his kingdom because of it.

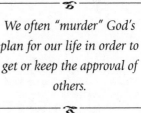

We often "murder" God's plan for our life in order to get or keep the approval of others.

God brought David into Saul's life to minister to him. Saul recognized the anointing and favor of God on David's life. When the people showed approval of David, Saul became jealous—so jealous, in fact, that he repeatedly tried to kill David. His need for approval was so great he was even willing to murder to prevent someone else from having more approval than he did. Thank God few people let their need for approval go this far.

We may not try to murder people, but we often "murder" God's plan for our life in order to get or keep the approval of others. Saul tried to do both. He tried to murder David, but instead he "murdered" God's plan for himself and his kingdom. As a result, Saul ended up being killed himself after having already lost the opportunity to remain king.

11

Pressing Past Rejection

And whoever will not receive and accept and welcome you nor listen to your message, as you leave that house or town, *shake the dust
[of it] from your feet.* (Matthew 10:14, emphasis mine)

Jesus gave instructions to His disciples regarding the handling of
rejection. He told them to "shake it off." Basically He was saying,
"Don't let it bother you. Don't let it keep you from doing what I
have called you to do."

Jesus was despised and rejected (See Isaiah 53:3), and yet He
never seemed to let it bother Him. I am sure He felt pain just as
you and I do when we experience rejection, but He did not let it
prevent Him from fulfilling His purpose.

Jesus told His disciples not to be concerned about rejection because in reality, people who rejected them were really rejecting
Him:

He who hears and heeds you [disciples] hears and heeds Me; and he
who slights and rejects you slights and rejects Me; and he who

slights and rejects Me slights and rejects Him who sent Me. (Luke 10:16)

The Lord loves His children, and He takes it personally when anyone rejects them or treats them contemptibly. If you are a parent, you know how you feel when anyone mistreats your children. If you are like me, you actually feel their pain and will do anything possible to prevent it.

I recall when my daughter Laura changed schools in about the third grade. She had been attending a Christian school and was transferred to a public school. She experienced major rejection from the children at her new school. I drove by the playground one day about recess time and saw her sitting on a bench all by herself while all the other children were playing. She looked so sad and lonely that it broke my heart to see her.

She would cry in the evenings because she didn't understand why nobody liked her. There was no reason for the children not to like her. Rejection was something Satan used to make her feel bad about herself as a person. Laura was a Christian child, and she talked about Jesus freely. The devil did not like it, so he attacked her.

Rejection is one of Satan's favorite tools to use against people. The pain of rejection often causes people to function in fear rather than boldness. Laura soon learned that when she talked about Jesus, the other children made fun of her, and it adversely affected her for a long time.

A SOLID FOUNDATION

If we start our life rooted in rejection, it is equivalent to having a crack in the foundation of our house. The first home Dave and I built had a crack in the basement, and it caused periodic problems for years. Each time there were storms or heavy rains, the basement leaked, and anything in the path of the water flow got wet. We tried three or four different methods before we were finally successful in getting the crack totally repaired.

People who have experienced rejection in their life are somewhat like our house. Each time there is a storm in their life, everything is a mess, including them. They try different methods to find security, but nothing ever works. They may try people-pleasing to find acceptance. Often they become approval addicts. They live with the emotional pain of rejection—or the fear of being rejected, which is often worse than rejection itself.

A solid foundation is the most important part of a building. Without a solid foundation, the building won't last long. Everything else concerning the building is built on the foundation. If the foundation is weak or cracked, nothing that is built on it is safe. It could crumble or fall apart at any time, especially if stress is placed on it by something like a storm or an earthquake.

The Bible encourages people to build their lives on solid rock, not sand. The person who hears the Word of God and does it is like the man who, in building his house, dug down deep and laid a foundation upon the rock. When the flood waters rose up, the torrent broke against that house and could not shake it or move it, because it had been *securely* built or founded on a rock (See Matthew 7:24–27).

If we try to build our lives on what people say and think of us—how they treat us, how we feel, or our past mistakes—we are building on sinking sand. Before I experienced the healing power of Jesus Christ, my life was like a house built on shifting sand rather than solid rock. My foundation was weak. I was not secure, I did not like myself, and I was filled with guilt and shame from abuse. I was rooted in rejection, and every relationship I tried to build and every decision I tried to make was affected by it. I feared the pain of rejection and needed to learn that I could survive it if necessary.

By the grace and mercy of God, I traded that old cracked foundation for a solid foundation, one based on Christ and His love. I am now rooted securely in Him.

The apostle Paul prayed for the church that they would be rooted deep in God's love:

> May Christ through your faith [actually] dwell (settle down, abide, make His permanent home) in your hearts! May you be rooted deep in love and founded securely on love. (Ephesians 3:17)

Think about your beginning in life, because it represents your roots. Did you get a good start in life? If not, thank God you can be uprooted and replanted in Christ. You may not have had a good beginning, but you can definitely have a good finish!

THE ROOT OF REJECTION AND ITS RESULTS

The beginning of any relationship represents its roots. A marriage has roots, a beginning or starting point. Dave and I did not get off to a good start because of all the emotional problems I had at the time. Our first several years were very rough. After I realized I needed help, it took several more years to repair all the damage I had done in the first few years of our marriage. Things got better little by little, but we both had to be patient and refuse to give up.

Dave and I were recently talking about our ministry and what a solid foundation it is built on. From the beginning we made sure we did things with excellence, maintained integrity, and kept the strife out of our life and ministry. We worked patiently with our employees to build into them the same principles that we had adopted and applied to our own lives and ministry. At this time we have our office in the United States, plus offices in South Africa, Australia, Brazil, Canada, England, India, Russia, and the Middle East. How can we possibly keep up with so much? We have a solid foundation, one that is built on God, His Word, and His principles. Had we not taken the time and effort necessary to build

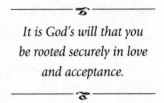

It is God's will that you be rooted securely in love and acceptance.

a good, strong foundation, we could not maintain such a massive work.

Foundations are extremely important. How is yours?

Are you rooted in shame, or rejection? Were your roots established in fear? It is God's will that you be rooted securely in love and acceptance; if you are not, you need emotional healing.

The word *reject* can be defined as to refuse, to throw away without value. Absolutely none of us want to feel like we are being thrown away as if we have no value. We all want to be noticed and accepted.

The word *root* can be defined as the starting point, the first growth from the seed. Seeds are buried and germinate, and roots develop and burrow down into the ground before the branches and fruit are seen above the ground. The quality of all fruit is affected by the roots that provide them support and nourishment. I have learned that rotten fruit equals rotten roots, and good fruit equals good roots. When we see bad fruit in our own life or other people's lives, we should realize it is coming from a bad root.

When people display bad behavior, rarely do they understand why they behave the way they do. If they cannot understand it, they certainly cannot change it. For many years of my life when I behaved badly, people said to me, "Why do you act that way? Why do you respond that way?" Their questions frustrated me because I did not have the answers. I knew my behavior was odd, confusing, and unstable, but I didn't know what to do about it. Most of the time I just blamed it on someone else or made excuses. I responded defensively to anything that even remotely seemed to be in disagreement with me. I did so because I already felt so wrong about myself that I couldn't face being wrong about anything else.

I responded fearfully to many situations, some of which made no sense at all. For example, if Dave would pull into someone's driveway to turn the car around, I became frantic, especially if he had to wait for other cars to pass by behind us before he could complete his turn. I said things like, "You shouldn't turn around in other people's driveways; the homeowners won't like it!" Or, I might say, "Hurry up and get out of here!"

Dave would say in bewilderment, "What is wrong with you? I'm just turning the car around. People use other people's driveways to turn around all the time."

For many years I did not understand why I reacted the way I did until God showed me that I was reacting to the situation based on how I thought my father would have felt about someone turning around in his driveway, which would have been angry. I was afraid the homeowners would come out the front door and yell at us the way my father would have done. I had such a deep-seated fear of rejection in my life that it caused me to react fearfully to many situations that seem very ordinary to an emotionally healthy person.

There were other similar situations that I reacted to based on past experience. I had no frame of reference other than the way I was raised. I had rotten, diseased roots, and therefore, I had bad fruit.

Do you have any behavior in your life that seems really weird? If so, have you ever wondered, "Where did that come from?" or "Why do I act that way?" I hope it helps you to realize that your fruit is a product of your roots. If you have bad roots—roots that were sown in rejection—you will need to be uprooted out of that bad soil and replanted in the love of God and the truth in His Word. The good news is, "There is hope." If you feel trapped in behavior that you don't understand, do not despair. The Holy Spirit will guide you into all truth. He will help you stop reacting to old situations and teach you to act on God's Word. He will give you an entirely new root system, one that will produce good fruit for His kingdom.

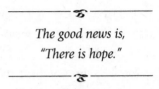

The good news is, "There is hope."

The Bible states in John 3:18 that for those who believe in Jesus there is no judgment, no condemnation, and no rejection. Jesus gives us freely what we struggle to earn from people and never seem to get: freedom from judgment, condemnation, and rejection!

When I became a student of God's Word, I started really desiring change in my behavior. Sometimes I was successful in cutting off one type of bad fruit (behavior), but another would immediately pop up, which frustrated me even more. I felt that no matter how hard I worked to get rid of one thing, another one took its place. It really helped me when I finally understood that my bad fruit was coming from a bad root. Another way of saying it is that my unacceptable outward behavior was coming from something unacceptable inside me.

My thoughts were wrong: about people, myself, circumstances, my past, my future, et cetera. I was very insecure, but I masked my feelings in a phony, bold approach to life that actually caused me to come across to others as harsh and hard. At that time I didn't understand why most people seemed to be offended by me, but now I do.

Have you ever been around people who outwardly seemed to "have it all together," so to speak, yet you just knew deep down inside that something was not right about them?

I recall a man (I'll call him Joe) who was a slick talker. He could have sold honey to bees. He appeared to be very confident. Actually, he was so confident that he was frequently accused of being haughty and prideful. He could cry crocodile tears at just the right moments, appearing to have tremendous compassion for hurting people. He had great vision and progressive ideas and was able to motivate people.

Joe became involved in youth ministry, and soon many teenagers admired him and became dependent on him for advice and teaching. Everything about him *appeared* to be right, but something about him *felt* wrong. The young people were almost too attached to him. They bordered on idolizing him.

On the outside, in public, everything seemed to be fine, but at home, behind closed doors, his marriage was in serious trouble. He, of course, always blamed it on his dysfunctional wife. She had deep problems, he said. As it turned out, he became involved with one of the young girls in the youth group, and a trail of lies a mile long was uncovered that had existed for years.

This man's father was one who was difficult to please, so Joe always felt rejected by him. His father pressured him to be something he did not know how to be. Therefore he had deep-rooted insecurities. He was trying to function in leadership with a deep root of rejection in his own life.

On the surface he appeared to be anything but insecure, yet he was totally insecure. His security and confidence came from other people's dependence on him, like the youth he oversaw, and from being able to do well in business. Like so many of us, he was deriving all his sense of worth and value from outward things rather than from God.

Many people today have developed phony personalities in which they function. They pretend to be whatever they think people will admire. It is very important to have discernment where these people are concerned. When things *appear* to be right, but they *feel* all wrong down deep inside, I recommend not getting involved too quickly. Take time to see how people act in all kinds of situations. They may talk a good game, but see if their walk

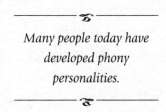

Many people today have developed phony personalities.

matches their talk. People may have problems that are not their fault, but we cannot allow ourselves to be deceived by them. We cannot help them if we merely get into their trap with them.

After Joe fell into sin and was exposed, numerous people said they had realized for a long time that something just wasn't right where he was concerned. They had caught him in lies, but just let it go; they had thought he might be involved with the young girl in question, but they didn't want to accuse him; they had recognized that he fed on being the center of attention, but they overlooked it.

Once again we see a situation in which nobody wanted to be the one to confront a situation, and as a result, in the end many people were devastated emotionally and spiritually. Instead of exposing and confronting the wrongs they saw in Joe, people simply got into his trap with him, and in the process they became trapped themselves. Joe was like a spider weaving a web. Everyone got swept up in his charismatic personality, and before they knew it they were caught.

No matter how good things may look outwardly, if they are not right on the inside, sooner or later they will be revealed on the outside. Anything we don't deal with will ultimately deal with us.

THE FEAR OF REJECTION

The fear of rejection is often worse than actual rejection. Fearing rejection all the time is more tormenting than just dealing with it on the occasions when it does occur. Fearing it certainly won't prevent it and may actually open a door for it.

The fear of rejection is rampant, and loneliness is one of the most dangerous and widespread problems in America today. It is well-documented that loneliness has reached epidemic proportions and continues to spread. Lonely people share a common symptom: a sense of despair at feeling unloved and a fear of being unwanted or unaccepted.

The fear of rejection leads people into superficial relationships or isolation. It affects their ability to give and receive love. The fear of rejection may cause a person to withdraw his love from someone he genuinely cares for. Why? He would rather reject than be rejected. He would rather think that ending the relationship is his choice rather than the other person's. Remembering past rejection, people often fear becoming too close. They think about how they would feel if they were rejected and believe the pain would be too much to bear. They pre-

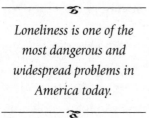

Loneliness is one of the most dangerous and widespread problems in America today.

fer the pain of isolation and loneliness, which only leads them to a greater need for acceptance.

In our own lives, we observe a vicious cycle. We want acceptance, but we fear rejection, so we isolate ourselves. Isolation only increases our need for acceptance, so we try to reach out to others, and end up repeating the same cycle again and again.

The fear of rejection only exists because we base our self-worth on the opinions of others rather than our relationship with God. Most of those who are critical of us are actually people who have a poor self-image themselves. They avoid the pain of how they feel inside by finding things wrong with other people and concentrating on their imperfections. Hurting people hurt people. It may help you to remember this truth when you are experiencing rejection or criticism. No wonder God tells us to pray for our enemies. They are in much worse condition than we are!

When I was growing up, I noticed that my father accused other people of doing things he was doing himself. He especially accused people of being sexually promiscuous. This behavior always amazed me because I knew how he was. Not only was he sexually abusing me, but I was aware of his unfaithfulness to my mother with other women. He also frequently accused people of being phony and hypocritical, while he lived a lie. He was suspicious of everyone and trusted nobody, and it was because he was so deceptive himself. In his thinking he transferred all of his own problems onto other people, accusing them of what he was doing while making excuses for himself.

When people cannot feel honorable about themselves they always find fault with other people.

THE RESULTS OF REJECTION

Let's take a look at some of the results of a life that has been rooted in rejection.

INSECURITY

Insecurity is the number one problem caused by a root of rejection. People who have been rejected do not feel valuable, and that makes them feel vulnerable and unsafe. They fear the pain of being rejected again, so they develop ways to protect themselves from rejection. As we have seen, they may do things like isolate themselves. After all, they cannot get hurt if they don't get involved with anyone. They may become people-pleasers, thinking that if they please people all the time, they will avoid the pain of rejection. They may become caretakers. They may think that if they take care of people and are needed, then they will not experience the pain of rejection. Actually they probably don't *consciously think* any of these things, but avoiding the pain of rejection is the motivating factor in many of their decisions.

> *Don't let the way other people treat you determine your worth and value.*

Insecurity is a psychological disturbance of epidemic proportion in our society today. *Insecure* can be defined as being uncertain, lacking in confidence, or shaky. God wants us to be the exact opposite of all these things. He wants us to be certain, confident, and solid, even when people reject us. Don't let the way other people treat you determine your worth and value.

The Bible teaches us in Isaiah 54:17 that security is part of our inheritance as children of God. It actually says peace, righteousness, security, and triumph over opposition are our heritage from the Lord.

REBELLION

Rebellion is frequently rooted in rejection. Rebellious people have experienced the pain of rejection. These people are angry, and their anger is an inner rage that manifests itself in rebellion. They are fed up with being pushed around, and they aren't going to take it anymore!

POVERTY

It's true: A life of poverty can also be the result of rejection. If people have a poverty image, they do not see themselves as capable of having or enjoying the finer things of life. They admire what others have, but automatically assume they could never have them. They won't even try for the better jobs, because they feel they are not worthy to have them.

I know people who will never have much of anything simply because of the way they feel about themselves. In conversation they say things like, "I will never own my own home," or, "I will never drive a new car," or, "I could never shop there, because it's not a discount store." When I have asked such people why they think they could not have these things if others have them, they respond by saying, "I'm just not in that class; those things are above me."

This type of thinking is all wrong. We are all just people; if we are in a certain class, it is because we have relegated ourselves to it or allowed someone else to do so. God has not assigned His children to an upper class, a middle class, and a lower class. The world

---
🕉
The promises of God are
for "whosoever will."

🕉

may think like that, but God does not, and we should not either. The promises of God are for "whosoever will." Whoever will believe in God and serve Him wholeheartedly can be blessed in any way that anyone else can be blessed. With God there are no distinctions, and He is not a respecter of persons (See Galatians 2:6; Acts 10:34).

Escapism

Escapism is another result we see among people with a fear of rejection. They create their own pleasant world through daydreaming. There is nothing wrong with a healthy daydream or two, but living in a pretend world to escape from the real one is a sign of real mental and emotional problems.

Workaholism

I once heard that 75 percent of all world leaders have been abused and have experienced severe rejection.[1] When I heard that statistic, I was amazed. It is simply because those who have been abused and rejected work harder than most people to accomplish something important so they will be accepted.

Their abuse and rejection may not have been from their parents; it may have come from a teacher, their peers, or a relationship that was important to them. But whatever its source, it drives them to accomplish something in life for which they hope to be admired and applauded. They feel that they have to prove something, and they spend their lives trying to do so.

I can relate to this scenario very well because I was a workaholic. I can still hear my father's voice yelling at me, telling me that I would never be any good and that I would never amount to anything. The more he yelled, the more determined I became to prove him wrong.

I will probably always be a hard worker, because I am motivated by accomplishment. Once I needed it to feel good about myself; now I just want to be fruitful in God's kingdom and for His glory. I don't like to waste my time. I have lived more of my life than I have left, so I want to make the rest of it count.

People with a painful past are often driven by a need to feel important, to gain acceptance, to attain a sense of security. We may succeed if we work hard, but it will never satisfy us unless God is behind our success. Ultimately we must know who we are in Him. We must be rooted and grounded securely in Christ and in His love (See Ephesians 3:17 and Colossians 2:7 KJV). We are made acceptable to God through the Beloved (Jesus) (See Ephesians 1:6 KJV). True acceptance is not found in our accomplishments, but in what Jesus has accomplished on our behalf.

> *I believe there are people who die much earlier than they should because they live under so much stress that it wears out their body.*

If we do not know this truth, we may well be in danger of working ourselves to death. I believe there are people who die much earlier than they should because they live under so much stress that it wears out their bodies. In general we are a driven people. Very few of us actually live balanced, healthy lives.

We are driven by many things that we will find in the end won't matter after all. The Bible teaches us that we brought nothing into the world, and we will take nothing out of it (See 1 Timothy 6:7). Nobody on his deathbed has ever said, "I wish I had spent more time at the office." I believe in working hard, but if we are addicted to work, or if we derive our sense of worth and value from it, we need help.

The writers of the Bible were led by the Holy Spirit to repeatedly tell us that our works will not gain us right standing with God. When we try to do right in life, it should be the result of knowing that we are loved, not an effort to gain love. We should do what we do for God, but not to get Him to do something for us.

People who derive their sense of worth and value from their accomplishments frequently talk about all they are "doing." They of course never take vacations, and even if they do, they work while on them. They even have a critical attitude toward those folks who like to enjoy life: they view them as lazy do-nothings, people who merely take up space and add very little to life.

They may have a martyr complex and become greatly offended when people don't notice and applaud all their efforts. The very fact that they seek recognition proves their motives are wrong. I truly pity workaholics. They have very little ability to enjoy life. As I have mentioned, more than likely they will make themselves sick or even shorten their life span. They don't take time to develop close relationships, and as a result they frequently end up lonely and burned out. The saddest thing I have ever seen is an old man in his eighties, knowing that he does not have long to live, and when he looks back at the life he has lived, all he has is regrets.

Actually, the list of possible results from a root of rejection is endless, so I won't detail anymore. But in the interest of jogging your conscience, here are a few I am aware of: self-pity, guilt, inferiority complex and poor self-image, fears of all types, hopelessness, depression, defensiveness, hardness, distrust and disrespect, competition and jealousy, and perfectionism. The main point is that you need to make right choices now so at the end of your life you will have nothing to regret. If you think you can be classified as insecure, rebellious, poverty-minded, escapist, or workaholic, you need to consider your motives, realize what is driving you, and make changes.

REJECTION AFFECTS PERCEPTION

How we see things is affected when we have a root of rejection in our lives. As I have mentioned, rejection-based people often perceive that they are being rejected when they are not. They may feel as if they are being mistreated when in reality they are not. They are very sensitive to the way people make them feel. They are actually overly sensitive.

Before God healed me in this area, I was very difficult to talk to. Unless Dave totally agreed with everything I said, I became upset. I perceived his disagreement as rejection. I would try to *convince* him to agree with me so I would feel "fixed." Dave, on the other

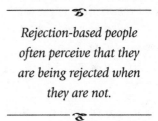

Rejection-based people often perceive that they are being rejected when they are not.

hand, would feel *manipulated*, as if he had no right to his own opinion about anything. Dave repeatedly said to me, "Joyce, I'm only giving my opinion. Why do you act like I'm attacking you?" I acted that way because I *felt* attacked!

This situation caused more than a few problems between Dave and me. I said repeatedly, "We just cannot talk about anything." To which Dave always responded, "Joyce, we don't talk anyway; you talk, and if I do anything other than listen and agree, you get upset."

If you are having trouble communicating with someone, then one or both of you may have the same problem I did. Healthy conversation between two people must include the right to be heard. I mean really heard. Do you listen, or just talk? I talked, and I wanted Dave to listen. I wanted him to agree with me. When he didn't, I stopped listening. At that point I started reacting out of my old wounds of rejection. I *felt* rejected even though he was not rejecting me. I perceived it that way, so it was that way for me.

I know God has changed me, because I don't respond to disagreement the way I once did. I can talk, and I can listen. I like agreement, but if I don't get it, I respect other people's right to their own opinion. I don't feel wrong just because they may not agree, but I am open to considering that I might be wrong. Even if my opinion turns out to be wrong, it does not mean something is wrong with me. Learn to separate your opinions and ideas from who you are as a person.

TALK TO YOURSELF

You can survive rejection, and you need to tell yourself that you can. I am suggesting that you actually talk out loud to yourself, telling yourself, "I can survive rejection." Also let the thought roll over and over in your mind, "I may not be accepted by everyone, but I can survive it."

We all fear rejection too much. Start believing you can survive it, if you need to do so. Jesus was rejected, and He survived. You can too! Value the unconditional love of God more than the conditional approval of people, and you will overcome rejection.

When I say you will survive, I don't mean that you will just barely make it. I mean that rejection really will not bother you at all. You just need to develop a new attitude toward it. When people have rejected me in the past, I have been hurt and let their attitude toward me control my thoughts for days afterward. When Dave has been rejected, he has simply said, "That's their problem, not mine." What was the difference between him and me? Dave was secure, and I was insecure. It is just that simple! I relied too much on what people thought of me, and Dave didn't care what people thought of him. He has told me that he cannot do anything about what people think; all he can do is be himself.

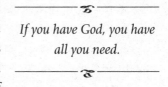

If you have God, you have all you need.

If you have had problems in these areas, stop torturing yourself with concern about what people think. You can survive rejection. You will live through it, and when people are finished thinking something unkind about you, they will go on to someone else. You will have the rest of your life left to live, and you can live it without them. If you have God, you have all you need. If He knows you need anything else, He will provide that also (See Matthew 6:8, 33–34).

I mentioned earlier in the book that some very unkind newspaper articles were written about us. I contacted a man I knew who owns a magazine and has been in the publishing and newspaper business for many years. I asked him what he thought we should do about the situation. He said, "If I were you, I would ignore it; the whole thing will blow over, and next week they will be picking on someone else." Sure enough, he was right.

We are not responsible for our reputation anyway. God is! So relax and keep saying to yourself, "I can survive rejection. I am not addicted to approval." Say it over and over until you believe it and are no longer bothered by the way people treat you. When Satan knows he cannot hurt you with rejection, he will stop working through people to bring that type of pain into your life.

In this part of the book, we've looked at some things we must change about ourselves as we begin to break the cycle of approval addiction. In the next section we will focus on some final important truths regarding our wholeness in God and where we need to be headed in our lives. There is good news for us if we're willing to take those steps!

PART

Breaking the Pattern
for the Future

Breaking Controlling Powers

*I*t is offensive to God when we let other people control us. He sent Jesus, His only Son, to purchase our freedom with His life. The Bible says we have been purchased with a price (See 1 Corinthians 6:20), and that price is the precious blood of God's only, dearly beloved Son.

If you are letting someone control your life—intimidate you, manipulate you, and cause you to do what you know in your heart is not right—then you need to break those controlling powers. It is not God's will for us to be controlled by anybody except His Holy Spirit, and even that decision He leaves up to us. God won't even force His will on us, so we certainly should not let anyone else do it.

Approval addicts almost always end up being controlled and manipulated by other people. Satan always sends someone along their way who is a "user." A user is someone who deviously takes advantage of people for his own benefit without any concern for others.

People who are being controlled are not confronters, and those who are controllers don't like being confronted. These two types of dysfunctional people play on each other's weaknesses. One enables the other.

THE ENABLER

We need to take some time to discuss the person who is an enabler. We can actually enable people to stay in bondage by continuing to give in to their demands instead of choosing to do what we believe is right for us as individuals.

People will take advantage of you, if you let them. They will be used by Satan to draw you away from what you should be focused on, which is God's will for you. The most vital thing for any Christian is prompt, hearty obedience to God. As we have already established, one cannot be a God-pleaser and a people-pleaser. The two will ultimately end up diametrically opposed to one another.

A woman who attended many of our conferences claimed to have an abusive past that was quite horrible. In our meetings, the woman displayed very disturbing behavior. She was disruptive. She would fall onto the floor, curl up in a fetal position, become wildly emotional when touched, and have to be literally carried out of the meeting.

We always had several people minister to her the best they could, but this pattern continued again and again. I began to dread her arrival any time I heard she was coming. I felt my heart sink when I saw her.

At times I felt bad about my negative feelings. I felt I should help her, but I honestly did not know what to do for her. There were times when she seemed as sane as anyone else, yet at other times she was quite out of control. Or as I discovered later, she was in control! She was not in control of herself, but she was controlling my meetings and my staff with her behavior.

One afternoon as I taught God's Word to a crowd of several thousand people, this woman began to act the same way she had in the past, only this time she fell out of her chair and lay on the floor between two rows of seats. The attention of everyone for several rows around her was on her. Our staff workers had to get

The most vital thing for any Christian is prompt, hearty obedience to God.

between the rows and try to minister to her. Finally they carried her out again as they had done previously. This of course totally disrupted the meeting. They took her to a private room and prayed for her, but nothing changed.

One of the women who was trying to help her felt in her heart that the woman was putting on an act to get attention, so she took a bold step. She said, "Okay, lady, you can lie here as long as you want. There will be an usher outside the door, but I am going back to my seat; I don't want to miss any more of the teaching." She walked out of the room, stood in a hallway, and watched to see what the woman would do. When the woman thought nobody was looking, she got up, walked out the door, and left the building.

The woman was manipulating us to get attention. She had been abused in her past, and she did need help, but at that particular time she was using us, and we were not helping her. As long as we continued to cater to her bizarre behavior, we were enabling her to remain in her trap. Confronting her was the kindest thing we could have done.

At times we feel we are being mean if we confront people who have problems, when in reality "tough love" is what Jesus often used to set people free.

Although Jesus had compassion for hurting people, He never merely felt sorry for them. And whenever possible he helped them help themselves. He instructed them to take some particular action, and frequently His instructions were shocking. For instance, He told a crippled man to rise, take up his bed, and go home (See Matthew 9:6). He told a man who had just received a report that his daughter was dead not to be afraid (Mark 5:35–36). When Jesus saw a blind man, He spat on the ground, made some mud by mixing dirt with it, and then rubbed it on the blind man's eyes. He then instructed the man to walk to the Pool of Siloam and wash himself in it; when the man did as Jesus had commanded, he was able to see (See John 9:1–7).

> *Jesus often told people to do things that were not only surprising, but were seemingly impossible.*

We see that Jesus often told people to do things that were not only surprising, but were seemingly impossible. How could a crippled man rise, take up his bed, and walk? After all, he was a cripple. How could a man who had just received a report of his daughter's death be expected not to fear? How could a blind man see to get to a certain pool of water when he was blind? Instead of merely feeling sorry for these people, Jesus moved them to action. He helped them get their minds off of themselves and their problems, and He motivated them to do something about them. Jesus was *moved* with compassion (See Matthew 9:36 KJV). He was moved to do something besides enable people to stay the way they were.

When Martha wanted Jesus to instruct her sister Mary to get up and help her work, Jesus told Martha that she was anxious and worried about too many things and that Mary was doing what was right in worshiping Him (See Luke 10:38–42). Jesus was straightforward, and He did not enable anyone to remain in deception.

When we fail to confront people who are controlling us, we enable them to stay the way they are.

MAKE YOUR OWN DECISIONS

Don't allow other people to make your decisions for you. You are being very unwise (foolish) if you let others make your choices. The Bible does say there is safety in many counselors (See Proverbs 11:14). It is a good thing to consider what others say, but the final choice must be yours. As the saying goes, "To thine own heart be true"; otherwise, there can be no real happiness.

Being controlled and manipulated steals your joy and peace. It ministers death to your spirit, your mind, your emotions, and every other part of your life. God said, "I have set before you life and death, the blessings and the curses; therefore choose life that you and your descendants may live" (Deuteronomy 30:19).

If you are going to choose life, then you must also choose to confront those people in your life who try to control you. People will actually respect you if you have borders in your life—areas you let them into and areas you do not let them into.

Dave and I run *Joyce Meyer Ministries* together as codirectors of the ministry. We both have strong personalities and frequently give one another advice. I receive advice from Dave in every area except what I am teaching in our conferences and on television. I know I must receive that information from God's Spirit—and not Dave or others—if it is to be anointed. I am a mouthpiece for God, and as such I must be led by Him in what I teach.

Dave has his own areas of expertise. He was in the engineering field prior to entering full-time ministry. When we built our ministry headquarters, he was very involved in the process because he understands that area. On a few occasions I tried to give him advice about something concerning the structure of the building, and he politely told me I should let him handle the building since that was his field.

We each receive advice from the other, but we have our borders, and we respect each other for it.

WHAT ABOUT SUBMISSION TO AUTHORITY?

The Bible teaches us to submit to authority (See 1 Peter 2:13). We are to submit to civil authority, church authority, employer authority, parental authority, and spousal authority. A rebellious attitude is one of the worst attitudes we can have. If we will not submit to man's authority, we will not submit to God's authority either.

However, the question always arises, "What if the authority I am under is unfair?" In some ways that is a hard question to answer simply because we frequently feel anything we don't want to do is unfair. God does not want nor does He expect us to be abused. But we may have to endure some things we feel are unfair.

The Bible says, "One is regarded favorably (is approved, acceptable, and thankworthy) if, as in the sight of God, he endures the pain of unjust suffering" (1 Peter 2:19). Unjust things may happen to us in this life, but God is just, and He will always make wrong things right, if we are patient and put our trust in Him. Our suffering does not make God happy, but when we continue to do what is right even if it means we have to suffer, that does please God.

I believe the key phrase in this Scripture is "if, as in the sight of God." In other words, we should endure the pain of unjust suffering for God, not necessarily because we want to. The verse prior to the one I quoted above is specifically talking about submission to authority that may be unkind and unreasonable. So if we endure unjust suffering from an authority that is unkind or unreasonable, for the sake of God and His kingdom, it pleases Him.

For example, a person may be led by the Holy Spirit to remain on a job where he is not treated fairly in order to be an example to unbelievers of the proper way to behave in such a situation. Or a person may be the only

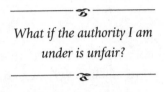

What if the authority I am under is unfair?

believer in Jesus Christ at his company, and the Holy Spirit may lead him to remain there in order to be a light in an otherwise dark place. All too frequently we are more concerned about our own personal comfort than we are about bearing good fruit for the kingdom of God. If being in the will of God means enduring some personal suffering or discomfort, we should not be afraid of it. Anything we do for God ultimately brings a reward. God always vindicates us and brings justice into our lives, but there are times when we must endure things that seem unfair at the moment.

There are also times when we should not endure; instead, we should confront. Discerning when to endure and when to confront is the real key to success and fulfillment in this area. I cannot give you exact direction on this subject. There is a time to do nothing and a time to do something. Each of us must seek God and be sensitive to follow His leading.

Some people are so timid, they endure longer than they should. They become a doormat for other people to walk on. As a result, they spend their lives being mistreated. Other people confront too quickly and too often. These people need to learn the dynamics of standing still and waiting on God.

Love is the highest law in God's kingdom.

People may think they are free when they refuse to submit to anyone, but they are actually in great bondage. True freedom is being free not to exercise a freedom if exercising it would not be good for all concerned. Love is the highest law in God's kingdom, and the apostle Paul stated in Romans that if what we do causes our brother to be pained or hurts his feelings, then we are not walking in love (See Romans 14:21). Paul also said he was free to do anything he wanted to do, but he was also free to discipline his personal desires for the good of the kingdom (See 1 Corinthians 6:12 and 9:22).

As Christians, we may say we are free to do whatever we want to; however, when it comes to living in community with others, this type of philosophy simply does not work. When one person in a group or society controls everyone else, it is called a dictatorship, not a family or a community. The only one who thinks he is happy is the dictator, and even he eventually discovers he is not happy either. God created us to live and work together in love and unity; without love and unity nothing else will ever work properly.

Let's look at some of the areas in which we are often challenged by negative authority.

WORK

When a boss demands so much of an employee that it is ruining his home life, his spiritual life, and perhaps his health, that employee is not being rebellious if he confronts the boss and states plainly what he can and cannot do. He actually would be guiltier if he did not confront than he would be if he did confront.

God expects a person to put his marriage, his family, his home, his spiritual life, and his health before his job. If he loses his job as a result of proper confrontation, then God will help him get a better one. It is sad when a person lives in so much fear of the loss of money and reputation that he allows himself to lose his health, the respect of his family, and a good relationship with God. If you have been allowing someone to control you, you should ask yourself what price you are paying to have that person's approval.

As I mentioned previously, I once worked for a man who required way too much from his employees. He was a Christian leader, and I respected him greatly. In the beginning, I just assumed that whatever he told me to do must be what God wanted me to do. But after a period of time I began to realize that my life was seriously out of balance because of trying to meet all of my boss's requirements in order to keep my job.

If you don't want to pay the price, then don't play the games.

I regret to say I let the situation deteriorate to the point that I was sick, and my marriage and children needed some serious attention. I had the approval of my boss, but I was out of God's will.

We can usually look back and see what we did wrong in the past easier than we can see what we are doing wrong while we are caught up in the emotion of the actual event. But, at least we can learn from our mistakes and not do the same foolish thing twice. I learned a lesson from this situation that has been beneficial to me at many other times in my life: When we let our lives get out of balance, we will always pay a price somewhere along the line. If you don't want to pay the price, then don't play the games you have to play in order to have everyone's approval.

CHURCH

When a pastor or other spiritual leader tries to "hear from God" for all his people about their decisions, he is being spiritually abusive. We all have the Holy Spirit, and we can all hear from God for ourselves. That does not mean we never need advice, because we do. But some people get way out of balance in this area.

Dave and I once had a pastor who thought the people in his congregation should not even sell their houses and move unless they asked him if he felt it was the right decision and the right time for them to make it.

This type of attitude is of course controlling and totally unscriptural. As far as I am concerned, this man was insecure and wanted people coming to him for everything so he would feel important. This same man also told my husband that he was making a mistake by letting me teach a Bible study in our home. He said my husband should be teaching it. There was only one small problem: God had given the gift of teaching to me, not to my husband. Dave tried to teach for a period of time, and I tried to keep quiet. Neither of us was happy or successful in our efforts!

Well-meaning people may try to tell you what you should do, but that does not always mean they are right. Dave and I would have missed an opportunity to share the gospel with millions of people worldwide had we listened to that pastor. He may have been sincere, but he was sincerely wrong.

Home

Parents must know when to let go of their children. Nothing is worse than parents who are still trying to run the lives of their grown children. Parents should not do that, but the children must not allow it. Both have a responsibility. There are times when Dave and I give our children advice, and I am sure there are times when they don't want it. We may tell them what we think, but we don't try to make them do it. We realize they must be free to make their own decisions and deal with their own consequences. If they give any indication that they really don't want our advice in a specific situation, we then keep our advice to ourselves, which is the right and proper thing to do.

Even if you are sure your child is making a mistake, you may not be able to do anything about it. Sometimes children learn more from the mistakes they make than from anything else.

Husbands and Wives

Because it so often comes up in issues of authority and submission, I want to quickly address this. In the Bible, wives are told to submit to their husbands "as unto the Lord" (Ephesians 5:22 KJV). This has been a big problem for many women, especially in our society today when women are fighting for equal rights. Women are equal with men; the Bible never says they aren't. But God is a God of order (See 1 Corinthians 14:33), and there can never be order unless someone is ultimately in charge. Someone has to have final authority to say what will and will not be done, especially when there is disagreement.

Women are not to be abused or controlled by their husbands. If a man dominates his wife—if he gives her no money, tells her what to wear, allows her no friends, refuses to let her go to church or read Christian books, et cetera—then I believe he is out of order, and she needs to confront him. That is quite different from being asked to do something she does not want to do. Doing things we don't want to do is part of life. The Bible tells us to adapt and adjust to others in order to maintain peace in our relationships (See Romans 12:16). Between two people or in a group of people there should be give and take; when there is not, it can easily become a situation in which one person controls everyone else. This is not right!

> *Between two people or in a group of people there should be give and take.*

As a wife, learning to submit to Dave's authority and be respectful to his opinions was very difficult for me. The pain I experienced in my past as a result of my father's controlling nature left me with an unhealthy perspective about the subject of submission. There were many times when I perceived (or I felt) Dave was trying to control me, when in fact that was not the case at all. If he even had an opinion that varied from mine, I felt threatened. If he ever actually told me he did not want me to do a certain thing I wanted to do, I responded by shouting, "If you think you're going to control me, you need to think again!"

With God's help I finally realized that my fear of Dave's trying to control me actually made me controlling. I am eternally thankful to the Holy Spirit for showing me the truth that has set me free to be submissive to authority—and thankful that Dave stayed with me long enough for me to learn.

Once again, submit to authority, but don't be controlled. If you are a person in authority, be authoritative, but don't be a controller. I have tried to learn not to be a "bossy boss." I pray for balance in these areas. They are not always easy to discern, but God's Spirit will guide us if we let Him. When you do make mistakes, which we all do, admit them and learn from them.

CHARACTERISTICS OF A CONTROLLER

If you are being controlled, the controller is likely someone you love and respect, or at least someone you liked and respected at one time. You may have lost your respect for the person because of the control but are so caught up in the cycle that you do not know how to break free.

The controller may be someone you need, and the controller knows it. It could be someone who supports you financially, and you don't know what you would do if that person were not in your life. It could be someone you feel indebted to for some reason, someone who has done a lot for you in the past—and who regularly reminds you of it. It could be someone you hurt in the past, and now you feel that you owe that person the rest of your life.

The controller may be someone you are afraid of. That was the case with my father and our relationship. You may be afraid of personal harm or loss, as when parents threaten to take children out of their will and not leave any of their money or possessions to them if they don't do everything they want them to do.

The controller may be someone who was controlled in childhood, and now he is functioning in learned behavior. It may be a proud, selfish, or lazy person (someone who wants and expects everyone else to serve him).

The controller may be a deeply insecure person who feels better about life when he is in control. He may need the number-one position to feel safe.

CHARACTERISTICS OF THE PERSON BEING CONTROLLED

The person who is most likely to be controlled is someone who has always been controlled, so that it is a habit, a way of life. Such a person is not accustomed to making his own decisions. It may be an insecure, fearful, or timid person who has never practiced confronting anything or anybody in life. His excuse is, "I don't like to confront." My answer is, "We all have to do things we don't like to do."

A person who is controlled may be confused about submission to authority. He may not be able to tell the difference between true godly submission and a wrong type of demonically instigated control. It would help him to remember that the devil controls; God leads!

The controlled person may have a poor self-image.

The controlled person may have a poor self-image. He may think so little of his ability that he assumes everyone else is always right, and he is always wrong. Anytime anyone disagrees with him, he may instantly shut down inside and submit. The person may be a neurotic individual who feels he is at fault in every conflict.

The controlled person may be dependent on others for care, finances, a place to live, employment, companionship, et cetera. The controlled person may have done wrong at one time and now feels he owes a debt to the controller, so he allows the control to continue.

CHARACTERISTICS OF CONTROL

There are two main characteristics of control. I want to address both of them.

Emotional Control

Emotional manipulation is one of the most evident and powerful characteristics of control. Tears, rage, and silence (especially silence as a form of rejection) are all methods frequently used by controllers to control others.

Perhaps both sets of parents want the newlyweds to spend the holidays with them. Controlling parents may use silence, rage, tears, or anger to get their way. They may remind the couple of "all the money" they gave the couple. This, of course, makes the couple feel indebted, in which case the parents really did not "give" them anything. True giving has no strings attached by which the persons who receive the gift can be pulled in whatever direction the giver wants them to go.

On the other side, parents who are behaving properly will allow the couple the freedom to make decisions for themselves; they will not pressure them. If they are Christian parents, they will probably pray for God to lead them and their children, and then go on about their business, trusting God to work it out. Parents who apply the least amount of pressure may not always get the children for the holidays, but they will receive the most love, admiration, and respect from them.

Although I was deceived about the true nature of my actions, I tried emotional manipulation for years. Every time Dave did not do what I wanted him to do, I got angry, became silent, cried, pouted, displayed a pitiful attitude, and cleaned house or worked continually at other chores hoping to make him feel guilty or sorry for me.

I am glad to say it did not work. No matter how I acted, Dave stayed happy and did what he felt he should do. Had I been successful in controlling him with my emotions, I might still be in the same trap. His lack of confrontation would have enabled me to continue my controlling ways. If you are a controller and really want to be brave, pray that God will lead people to confront you anytime you really need it. Then pray that you will receive it and not respond defensively with anger, accusations, and excuses.

VERBAL CONTROL

Other people may try to control with words of failure, defeat, unnatural obligation, guilt, criticism, and intimidation. Sometimes they use threats. For instance, they may threaten with loss of relationship (rejection). In other words, they may infer that if you don't do what they want you to do, they will no longer want to be in relationship with you. I believe many teenagers get involved in drugs, alcohol, and sexual misconduct because they are threatened with loss of relationships. We call it "peer pressure." It is actually control.

There are many methods of controlling others. If you are being controlled, learn to recognize the methods being used against you. If you are a controller, ask God to help you recognize your own methods of control. You cannot do anything about something you don't recognize. Pray for truth; the truth will make you free!

SYMPTOMS TO WATCH FOR

If you are unable to interact with others without the controller making you feel tense and guilty that you are enjoying yourself, what you are experiencing is a symptom of being controlled.

Or perhaps you cannot make new friends without the controller becoming jealous and possessive. You feel you always have to "check in" with the controller before you do anything. You have no personal life of your own. You have to tell the controller everything, invite him everywhere, and get his opinion about everything.

Maybe you have the controller on your mind excessively. You live with a vague fear of what he will think or say about everything you do.

These are all signs of a crisis that must be addressed. Let's take a look at five important steps in gaining freedom from control.

I. RECOGNIZE

The first step to getting free from control is to recognize you are being controlled. Some people may think they are just keeping the peace. As Christians we can even believe we are obligated to keep peace at all costs. The Bible does teach us to be makers and maintainers of peace, to adapt and adjust to other people in order to have harmony:

> Live in harmony with one another; do not be haughty (snobbish, high-minded, exclusive), but readily adjust yourself to [people, things] and give yourselves to humble tasks. Never overestimate yourself or be wise in your own conceits. (Romans 12:16)

As Christians, we are to do everything in our power to keep the peace, but that does not mean we are to allow others to control us. Any Scripture taken to an extreme can create a problem. Operating in love, we are to do what is for the good and advantage of other people, but we must realize it is not good for other people if we let them control us.

2. ACT

Once you recognize you are being controlled, choose to do something about it. You must not let it continue—not only for your sake, but also for the sake of the controller. If you let it continue, you are enabling him, and you become as guilty as he is. A bad habit has been formed that needs to be broken. You probably *react* to the controller in certain ways, and you must learn to *act* on God's Word and instruction to you. This will take some prayer and determination. Don't be discouraged if it takes time. It has been said that it takes thirty days to make a habit and thirty days to break one. I would imagine by the time you have confronted the controller thirty times, you will be well on your way to developing a new set of relationship rules.

3. UNDERSTAND

As I have mentioned, you need to learn *how* the person controls you. Is it through fear, anger, silence, rage, tears, guilt, or threats? It is important to quickly recognize the control tactics and resist them immediately. The quicker you resist, the less likely you are to fall into the trap you are trying to break free from.

4. CONFRONT

Face the battle of confrontation. Realize that if you have let another person have his way all the time, he will not like it when you change. It may even be wise for you to discuss the situation with the other person. You might say something like, "You may not be doing it on purpose, but I feel you are controlling me. I need to have freedom in our relationship, and God has shown me that although you should not control me, I have been wrong in allowing it. I am going to make a change, and I realize it may not be easy for you. I love you, and I want our relationship to flourish, but from now on I will be following my own heart."

Don't even expect the person not to react adversely. Just as you have been addicted to approval, the controller is addicted to control. No addiction is broken without some fleshly reac-

No addiction is broken without some fleshly reactions.

tions. As I always say, "The flesh (the carnal nature of man) never dies without a fight."

You may be afraid to confront, but you must do so even if you have to *do it afraid!* If you stand firm, the controller will ultimately move from anger to respect. I have never had a relationship with people who allowed me to control them in which I respected them. I actually disrespected them for not confronting me.

You may fear losing the relationship, and that is a possibility. The only thing I can say is that you would be better off without the relationship than to spend your life being controlled and manipulated. If people have no interest in you unless they can control you, then they are not really interested in you at all. Don't let people use you.

5. PRAY

Don't try to make any of these changes without a lot of prayer. Timing is very important in situations like these. Pray for the people you need to confront, asking God to prepare their heart. Ask Him to make them aware of their actions even before you speak to them.

A WORD TO CONTROLLERS

Although most of this book is directed to those who are addicted to approval and in the process allow others to control them, I also know that some people reading the book are controllers themselves. It is possible to be both a controller and someone who is controlled. I had periods of time in my life when I was controlling anyone who would let me, and at the same time I was being controlled by someone else. In both cases I was out of God's will. You may be the same. For instance, you might be controlled by your boss and yet be controlling your family at home.

If you are not sure whether you are a controlling person, ask yourself the following question: How do I respond when I don't get my way? Do you usually become angry or try to convince others that your way would be best? Are you unhappy until you do get your way? Be honest in your answer, and you will be able to identify yourself quickly.

People have a right to make their own decisions. God wants us to be led by His Word and Spirit, not by outside forces. He also wants us to let others be led the same way. As a matter of fact, we should not only let others be led by God, we should encourage them and help them do it. When we want others to do something, and they seem unsure, instead of trying to convince them to do what we want them to do, we should tell them to pray about it, and then trust that God will show them what to do. We can encourage people to do things, but we should not manipulate them to get our way. As the saying goes, "If you really love others, set them free; if they really belong to you, they will come back on their own." True love means that we help a person make the right decision for all concerned, not just the right decision for us.

FIVE THINGS TO DO IF YOU ARE A CONTROLLER

If you have controlling tendencies, you need to do the following:

1. Admit it to yourself. Try saying out loud, "I am a controller."
2. Ask God to forgive you and to teach you to respect other people's rights.
3. Ask the people you have been trying to control to forgive you.
4. Encourage them to be honest with you about how they really feel about situations between the two of you. Ask the person to confront you when you get out of line.
5. Don't give up or get discouraged if your change takes time.

You must realize your controlling tendencies won't just disappear overnight. Even after you admit them and begin to recognize them, it will still take time to break free of them. Confessing our faults to one another breaks their power over us and has a freeing effect on all concerned (See James 5:16). Facing truth starts a healing process in our life. When I was in my healing process, I told my husband to let me know if I sounded disrespectful to him. I had a lifetime of bad habits to overcome, and I wanted all the help I could get.

You may think, as I did, you are protecting yourself by staying in control, but you are actually opening a door for the devil to destroy all your relationships and load you down with unbearable stress. Trying to control everyone

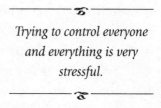

Trying to control everyone and everything is very stressful.

and everything is very stressful. I was relieved to finally discover I did not have to try to run the entire world. If you have been the great choir director of everything in your world, you need to retire.

Even if you have developed controlling tendencies because you were hurt in the past, it is still wrong. You may be a certain way because of the pain you have endured, but don't let it be an excuse to stay that way.

Not everyone who is controlling has abuse in his or her past. Some controllers just have very strong personalities and very definite ideas about how everything should be done. They are so strong about what they think and feel that they are not open at all to other people's opinions and thoughts. Others are just plain selfish. They are addicted to getting their own way, and they may have developed the bad habit of not respecting other people. Perhaps they were not corrected for these bad attitudes as children or were raised by parents who displayed controlling traits. Whatever the reason, one thing is for sure: they are not walking in love, and God is not pleased.

If you realize you have been controlling others, make a decision to let them be free to make their own decisions. If you don't agree with their decisions, refrain from showing displeasure. You might say, "I respect your right to choose; you are entitled to your own opinion."

Don't insist that everything be done your way. Don't get angry when others tell you no or don't seem to want to do what you want. Don't give people the "silent treatment" when they say no or confront you. Don't make them feel rejected. Tell them you respect them and realize they need to be free to follow their own heart. Tell yourself over and over, even repeating it out loud, "People have a right to make their own choices and have their own opinions and I should respect their right to do so." Say it until your attitude begins to change.

When I was in the process of overcoming controlling tendencies I frequently said quietly to myself, "Joyce, this is none of your business." I did this when I was tempted to get involved in something that no one had invited me into. We love to give our opinions and tell people what we think, but the truth is most people don't even really want to know what we think. (I have found that even when people ask me what I think, they normally just want me to agree with them so they feel better about their decision.)

Don't make plans for other people without checking to see if they want to do what you have in mind. Following the simple scriptural instruction to treat other people the way you want to be treated will solve all of the control problems (See Luke 6:31).

DON'T OVER-CORRECT YOUR PROBLEM

It is not uncommon upon discovering that we have been extreme or out of balance in an area to swing to the other side of extreme behavior in an effort to correct the situation. For example, when Kevin finally realized that Stephanie had been controlling him for years, he decided he was going to correct the situation. His decision was good but his methods were not. He became so determined that she would never control him again that he became overly aggressive toward her anytime she seemed to be anything other than totally compliant to his wishes.

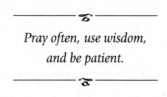

Pray often, use wisdom, and be patient.

In trying to make sure she never controlled him again, he ended up being the way she had once been.

They went to counseling sessions and Stephanie admitted her problem and sincerely wanted help. She needed to be confronted but Kevin became downright mean to her. Kevin finally saw that his methods were extreme and that he was trying to fix one problem but in the process was creating another problem. It took some time and effort but with God's help they learned to respect one another and have a balanced relationship.

Excess is the devil's playground. Anytime we become excessive in any area it becomes an atmosphere that Satan can work in. Strive to be in balance. If you realize you have been being controlled by someone you definitely need to take measures to regain your freedom, but don't let your response be emotionally driven. Pray often, use wisdom, and be patient. Don't go from being controlled to being so determined no one will ever control you again that you react to people in an out-of-balance manner. Likewise, if you have been a controller don't go to the opposite extreme and think you must never show any aggression at all.

Now that we have discussed taking positive steps toward freeing ourselves from negative control, let's look at ways we can use the pain we have experienced in the past to make a positive difference in our lives and the lives of others.

Using Your Pain

There is no way to get through life without experiencing pain. But it does not have to be wasted. After feeding the multitudes, Jesus told His disciples to gather up the fragments "so that nothing may be lost and wasted" (John 6:12). The Lord will make use of everything in your life if you let Him. Let your pain be someone else's gain. That's what Jesus did.

Jesus endured horrible pain as He hung on the cross paying for the sins of man. But His pain is our gain. God's Word teaches us that when we don't know how to pray as we should in a situation, the Holy Spirit comes to our aid. He knows the will of the Father in all things and pleads in behalf of all the saints according to and in harmony with God's will. Therefore we can be assured and know that *all* things work together for good for those who love God and are called according to His purposes (See Romans 8:26–28).

No matter what happens in our life, if we will keep praying and trusting God, keep loving Him and walking in His will to the best of our ability, He will cause everything to work out for good.

Whatever happened to us in the past may not have been good in and of itself, and it may have led to a struggle with acceptance and desire for approval, but because God is good, He can take a very difficult and painful thing and cause it to work out for our good and the good of others.

GOD'S PURPOSE IS BEYOND OUR COMPREHENSION

The only monument in the world built in the shape of a bug—to honor a bug—is located in Fort Rucker, Alabama. In 1915 the Mexican boll weevil invaded southeast Alabama and destroyed 60 percent of the cotton crop. In desperation, the farmers turned to planting peanuts. By 1917 the peanut industry had become so profitable that the county harvested more peanuts than any other county in the nation. In gratitude, the people of the town erected a statue and inscribed these words, "In profound appreciation of the boll weevil, and what it has done as the herald of prosperity."

The instrument of their suffering had become the means of their blessing.

God is a God of purpose. We may not always understand His purpose, but we can be sure He definitely has one. Something may initially look terrible to us, and yet all the while God intends to show His glory by working something good from it.

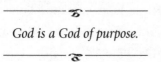

God is a God of purpose.

We see an example of this truth in the biblical account of the death of Lazarus as recorded in John 11:1–44. We are told that Lazarus was sick. His sisters Mary and Martha sent a message to Jesus saying, "He whom You love [so well] is sick"

(v. 3). When Jesus received the message, He said the sickness was not unto death but in order that God might be glorified. Instead of going to Lazarus and healing him, Jesus waited until he died. By the time Jesus arrived on the scene, Lazarus had been in the grave four days. Jesus raised Lazarus from the dead. He could have kept him from dying, but He let him die so people could see the miracle-working power of God and know that nothing is too hard for Him.

We wonder sometimes why God waits so long to come to our rescue or why He allows certain things to take place. We cannot always figure out what God is doing, or why He is doing it, but if we trust Him, He will make something wonderful from it.

HURT! HEALED! AND READY TO HELP!

Joseph was a man who was hurt by his brothers. We know from reading God's Word that Joseph's brothers were jealous of him. They hated him because his father favored him. They sold him into slavery and told his father that wild animals had killed him. He was taken to Egypt where he spent thirteen years in prison for a crime he did not commit (See Genesis 37–41).

But God was with Joseph, and he was able to interpret dreams. The ruler of all Egypt, Pharaoh, had a dream that Joseph interpreted, and he was released from prison. He went to work for Pharaoh, and once again was put in charge of everything. During a great famine, Joseph was in a position to save multitudes of people, including his father and his brothers who had treated him so cruelly.

This story is one of the most encouraging in the Bible. We see the power of a good attitude during hard times. We see that no matter where we are, God can give us favor. We see the power of forgiveness when Joseph was willing to feed his brothers who had hurt him so badly. The Bible says God's ways are past finding out (See Romans 11:33 KJV). We may not always understand, but we can trust.

Joseph had been hurt, but he was healed, and stood ready to help. His struggles had made him a better man, not a bitter man. Just think how different his life could have been had he refused to maintain a godly attitude all the way through his ordeal.

I am sure Esther was hurt when her life and plans were interrupted, and she was taken into the king's harem, which was not something a young Jewish maiden would have been happy about. When we read about people in the Bible, and the things they endured, we don't always think about the emotions they must have experienced. We read their stories almost as if they are fictional characters, but they were real people just like you and me. They went through all the same emotions we would go through in a similar situation.

> *We may not always understand, but we can trust.*

Esther was used by God to save her nation, but first He had to put her in an uncomfortable position. She had to live in a place she did not want to be and do things she did not want to do. (See the book of Esther.)

Ruth's husband died. I am sure that hurt her terribly. No doubt she was lonely, yet she chose to take care of her mother-in-law, an elderly woman named Naomi whom she accompanied to her foreign homeland. Once there, they had very little provision, and so Ruth had to glean in the fields in order for them to eat. She ended up marrying a man named Boaz, who was very wealthy. As a result, Ruth and Naomi were provided with everything they needed. In addition, by bearing children to Boaz, Ruth became part of the ancestral bloodline of Jesus. (See the book of Ruth and Matthew 1:5.)

My point in recounting these stories is that all of these people, and many others I don't have time to mention, suffered pain, received healing, and went on to help others.

Have you been hurt by someone or something? If so, you can make the same choice these people made. Don't spend your life angry and bitter—don't allow your emotional pain to imprison you in a lifelong struggle with approval. Receive healing and comfort from God, and then go on to help someone else. Don't waste your pain.

During World War II, Corrie ten Boom and her sister were held in a horrible concentration camp named Ravensbruck. They saw and suffered terrible torments including starvation and nakedness in below-freezing weather. Corrie's sister Betsie actually starved to death. During their time there, however, they continually encouraged other prisoners. They kept an attitude of praise, and eventually Corrie was released from the concentration camp through a clerical error.

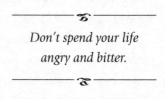

Don't spend your life angry and bitter.

After her release, she traveled worldwide telling of her experiences and the faithfulness of God. Her ministry surely became more powerful and effective than it would have been without her trials and suffering. Her life and ministry have been a comfort to millions.

One evening after preaching in Germany on God's forgiveness and how no sin is too great for God to forgive, she suddenly recognized a man coming toward her. He had been a guard at Ravensbruck, and one of the people who had tortured the prisoners. The man did not recognize Corrie, but he said he had heard her mention that she was a prisoner in Ravensbruck. He said, "I was a guard there, but have since gone on to become a Christian. I know God has forgiven me for the terrible things I did, but I am asking you for your forgiveness as well."

Corrie said that she immediately saw her beloved sister slowly starving to death, and felt at that moment that even though she needed forgiveness every day herself, she could not forgive this man. As she stood in front of him, she knew that she must forgive him although she did not know how she could. Everything she preached to others would be worthless if she could not forgive. Corrie said she knew it would have to be an act of her will, because nothing in her emotions wanted to do it. As she stood there, she told God, "I can lift my hand, I can do that much, but You will have to do the rest. You must supply the feelings." As she woodenly took the man's hand, she said that the power of God came rushing through her entire being, and she was able to say wholeheartedly, "I forgive you, brother!" "With all my heart, I forgive you." She said that she has never known God's love so intensely as she did at that moment.

Although Corrie had been badly hurt, she allowed God to heal her, and she went on to help others.[1]

As I have noted, I was abused and hurt very badly. When I was a young woman in my early twenties, I could never remember being happy or feeling really safe. I spent many years angry, bitter, and resentful. I am thankful that I learned to receive God's comfort and healing and that I am now able to help other people.

GOD IS LOOKING FOR EXPERIENCED HELP!

Have you ever needed a job, but every employment ad you read asked for someone with experience? You wanted a job but did not have any experience, and it frustrated you. I have been in that situation, and I remember thinking, "How can I get experience if nobody will give me a job?"

God also wants experienced help. When we go to work for God in His kingdom, He will use everything in our past, no matter how painful it was. He considers it experience. We have gone through some difficult things, and those things qualify us to help take someone else through them too. Even Jesus gained experience through the things He suffered:

Although He was a Son, He learned [active, special] obedience through what He suffered

And, [His completed experience] making Him perfectly [equipped], He became the Author and Source of eternal salvation to all those who give heed and obey Him. (Hebrews 5:8–9)

How could I be writing this book right now if I had not gone through some difficult things and gained some valuable experience? How could I teach others how to forgive those who have hurt them if I had not first had the experience of forgiving those who hurt me?

I encourage you to look at your pain from a different viewpoint. A right perspective can make all the difference in the world. Take a look at how you can use your pain for someone else's gain. Can your mess become your ministry? Maybe you have gone through so much that you feel you have enough experience to be a specialist in some area. I am a specialist in overcoming shame,

—————— ❧ ——————
Look at how you can use
your pain for someone
else's gain.
—————— ❧ ——————

guilt, poor self-image, lack of confidence, fear, anger, bitterness, self-pity, et cetera. Press past your pain and get your "master's degree" so you can work in the kingdom for the One Who is the Master of restoring hurting people.

THE BEST KEPT SECRET

Do not let yourself be overcome by evil, but overcome (master) evil with good. (Romans 12:21)

We overcome evil with good. I believe this truth is one of the most powerful weapons we possess, and the best kept secret. God wants everyone to know it, but Satan keeps us so entrenched in our problems and personal pain that few of us ever understand the dynamics of it. We can get Satan back for the painful things he has brought into our lives by being good to others. We overcome him (evil) by being good to other people. Actually, it is God Who overcomes Satan as we allow Him to work His good through us. Satan wants to use our pain to destroy us, but we destroy his plan by doing the opposite of what he expects.

Being good to someone else not only defeats Satan, it also releases joy in our own lives. Historically, people who have been hurt by someone frequently experience depression. I believe this is partially due to the fact that their attention is on their own pain instead of on what they can do to relieve someone else's pain. God has not called us to "in-reach," He has called us to "out-reach." When we reach out to others, God reaches into our souls and heals us. He is the only One Who can heal the brokenhearted and make the wounded better than new.

I call this "overcoming evil with good" principle a secret because so few of us seem to know it or follow it. When we are hurting, our natural tendency is to nurse our wounds. We may want to isolate ourselves and think about how pitifully we have been treated. I have discovered that when I am hurting, the best thing I can do is keep moving. While I am hurting, I just keep doing what I would be doing if I were not hurting. I go to work, I study, I pray, I go out and preach, I keep my commitments. I keep doing the good things God has given me to do, and I trust Him to take care of the evil things.

Do you see it? You can overcome evil with good just as the Bible says in Romans 12:21. Understanding this principle has been literally life changing for me, and I believe it can be for you, too.

OUR THINKING IS ALL WRONG

Our daughter Sandra shared that she was dreading seeing a certain individual because in the past that person had not been very pleasant to her. As she struggled with negative thoughts about the upcoming encounter, God spoke to her heart and said, "You don't need to be concerned about how others treat you; your concern should be how you treat them."

This message had a strong impact on Sandra's life as well as on mine. How true it is. We are so concerned about how we are being treated that we have little or no concern for how we treat others. We are afraid of being taken advantage of, especially if our experience with someone has been painful in the past. The fear and dread we feel probably makes us supersensitive to everything that is said or done. We may even misinterpret things and see them in a negative way because of our expectations. What we fear does come upon us, according to God's Word (Job 3:25).

You don't need to be concerned about how others treat you; your concern should be how you treat them.

I agree that it is difficult not to be concerned that others will treat us badly if they have done so in the past. That is why it is so important not to think about it at all. We are to deposit ourselves with God and trust Him to take care of us (See 1 Peter 4:19). He is our Vindicator (See Job 19:25), and as long as we behave properly toward others, including our enemies, God will bring a reward into our lives.

Because of what God had spoken to Sandra's heart, she approached the meeting with a totally different attitude. She concentrated on being nice to the person who had previously not been nice to her. She made an effort to be encouraging and to show interest in what interested the other person. She reported to me that the results were quite amazing. She spent several days with the individual in question, and never once did she feel mistreated in any way.

The Bible says we are to be "mindful" to be a blessing (See Galatians 6:10). That means that we are to have our minds full of ways we can help others. When our minds are filled with ways to be a blessing, we have no time to dwell on our personal problems. It gives God an opportunity to work on them for us.

GIVE AWAY WHAT YOU WANT

What do you want? If it is approval, then give approval to others. Make a special effort to make people feel valued and loved. Be aggressive in agreement. Often we are silent when we agree and verbal when we disagree. I find that the words "I agree" give confidence to people. If I have an opinion or an idea about something, it really increases my confidence level when my husband says, "I agree." I don't expect him to agree with me about everything, but when he does agree, it is really nice to hear it. I think hearing about the times when people do agree helps us better handle the times when they don't.

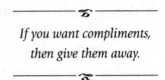

If you want compliments, then give them away.

If you want compliments, then give them away. Every time you think anything good about anyone, verbalize it. People cannot read your mind; your thoughts have power and may affect their confidence level in a minor way, but your words can really lift them up and encourage them.

All people need affirmation, especially those who have been emotionally wounded or hurt by someone. We have more power than we realize we do. We can help people! Right words spoken at the right time have the power to heal: "A man has joy in making an apt answer, and a word spoken at the right moment—how good it is!" (Proverbs 15:23).

Not only are right words spoken at the right time good for others, they are good for us. We experience joy in building others up. We are created by God to be a blessing. He told Abraham, "I will bless you and make you a blessing" (See Genesis 12:1–3). We are blessed in being a blessing.

God made you to be a blessing. Start being what you were made to be, and you will start receiving what you are meant to receive!

"I NEED HEALING"

You may be thinking, "I've been hurt, and I want to help others, but I need healing." I used this statement previously: "Hurt! Healed! And ready to help!" The healing is very necessary. There are lots of people in ministry who are trying to heal others, and they are wounded themselves. I call them "wounded healers." Many people hide from their own issues while trying to uncover someone else's. The blind cannot lead the blind—if they try to do so, they will both fall into a ditch (See Matthew 15:14). Trying to help others while ignoring our own problems never produces good fruit for anyone.

How does the healing come? We know how we got hurt. We have a vision to help others. But how does our own healing come? We need the help of the Great Physician. We need His presence in our lives. Spending time with God is the most vital thing we can do, especially when we have been wounded.

We must spend time reading and studying God's Word, because it has inherent power to heal. The Bible says we are to attend to God's Word because it brings health and healing to all of our flesh (See Proverbs 4:20–22). Our emotions and our mind are part of what the Bible calls "the flesh." According to Psalm 119:130 (KJV), the entrance of God's Word brings light, which is something many of us are missing. We don't always see what we need to do. Often we don't even see our own problems. We think everyone else has a problem, and if everyone else would change, everything would be fine. We need light from God to understand ourselves.

As I began my healing journey with God, His Holy Spirit started leading me into truth. Truth is another way to describe light. There were many things I did not understand. I didn't understand why I felt certain ways in certain situations or about certain types of people. My lack of light brought confusion in my life. It contributed to my negative feelings about myself. I didn't like many of my ways, but I could do nothing about them because I was in the dark. I felt trapped! I didn't like the things I did; I didn't understand them, but I kept on doing them.

I always disliked men who had strong personalities, which is really funny since I have a very strong personality myself. When God brought light into my life, I began to realize I was uncomfortable with a strong male authority figure because my father who abused me had a strong personality. I

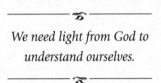

We need light from God to understand ourselves.

was responding to other men's personalities similar to my father's as I would have responded to him. I was always uncomfortable around my father, so I was uncomfortable around anyone like him.

The light God gave me helped me a great deal in relationships. For one thing, I stopped rejecting people just because they were men and had strong personalities. I had preferred to be around people who would let me take the lead; I had to be in control to be comfortable. Why? When God brought light into my life, I began to realize it was because I was *afraid* to let anyone else lead. I didn't trust they would have any real concern for my happiness.

I was not a mean person as the devil had tried to make me believe; I was just frightened. I had developed a complex system of ways to protect and take care of myself. I knew how to manipulate almost any situation to make sure no one took advantage of me. Yet I was tired of trying to protect and take care of myself all the time. I said I wanted someone to take care of me, but when anyone tried, I would not allow it. I wouldn't even let God take care of me. But His light set me free. Little by little He showed me things that opened my eyes and heart and allowed change to come.

All healing is a process that takes time, especially emotional healing. It is not all easy. Sometimes it is quite painful. Sometimes people have wounds that are still infected. The wound must be opened up and the infection taken out before they can heal properly. Only God knows how to do this and do it properly. Spending time with God in His Word and in His presence are the two main ingredients to being healed after being hurt.

HELP SOMEBODY ON PURPOSE

While you are letting God work in your own life, use your pain. Be aggressive in helping others. Don't wait to feel like it. Don't wait for some supernatural sign that God wants to use you. Just get started. God will use you in your world, with the people you are around in your daily life. What you make happen for somebody else, God will make happen for you. Every seed you sow into somebody else's life represents a harvest you will reap in your own life—especially in your pursuit to overcome approval addiction.

> *What you make happen for somebody else, God will make happen for you.*

Don't waste your pain. Let it be somebody else's gain!

CONCLUSION

Living Complete in Christ

*F*eeling that something is missing in our lives and not knowing what it is leaves us frustrated and continually searching. We become like the people God talked about in Jeremiah 2:13: those digging empty wells that have no water in them. We try first one thing and then another, but nothing quenches our thirst for whatever it is that is missing in our lives.

We might describe our feelings as being incomplete, yet the Bible says we are complete in Jesus:

> And ye are complete in him, which is the head of all principality and power. (Colossians 2:10 KJV)

> And you are in Him, made full and having come to fullness of life [in Christ you too are filled with the Godhead—Father, Son and Holy Spirit—and reach full spiritual stature]. And He is the Head of all rule and authority [of every angelic principality and power]. (Colossians 2:10)

To be complete means to be satisfied, filled up, assured. Without Christ, people are always searching, looking for something. They

> *When we believe, trust in, and rely on the Lord, we are blessed.*

feel incomplete. The sad thing is that most people don't know Jesus Christ is what they are looking for, so they try to fill up the emptiness in their lives with all sorts of other things.

We all want to feel satisfied. We all want contentment. We all want to know we are loved and accepted for who we are. We may think acceptance and approval from people will make us feel complete. However, the Bible teaches us that when we trust in man to give us what only God can give, we live under a curse; but when we believe, trust in, and rely on the Lord, we are blessed (See Jeremiah 17:5–8). The joy, peace, and fulfillment we seek come from being filled with God, and nothing else. They do not come from having a certain person in our lives, or from money, position, power, fame, accomplishments, or anything else. If you don't believe me, go ahead and try all the other things. You will ultimately come to the same conclusion we all do. You will admit that you are bankrupt as a person, that nothing you have tried has given you what you desire—a sense of fullness and completeness. Read the book of Ecclesiastes, which was written by Solomon. He was a man who tried literally everything to find this kind of deep inner completeness and satisfaction. Nothing he tried worked until he came full circle and realized that what he truly wanted had been available all the time. He wanted God!

Solomon began with God, but drifted away. He tried women, money, fame, power, labor, accomplishments, success, et cetera. Nothing worked! Listen to some of the things he said:

Vapor of vapors and futility of futilities, says the Preacher. Vapor of vapors and futility of futilities! All is vanity (emptiness, falsity and vainglory).

What profit does man have left from all his toil at which he toils under the sun? [Is life worth living?] (Ecclesiastes 1:2–3)

I have seen all the works that are done under the sun, and behold, all is vanity, a striving after the wind and a feeding on the wind. (Ecclesiastes 1:14)

I like the way Solomon said it. Trying to find fulfillment in anything the world has to offer is like chasing the wind. No matter how hard we chase after it, it always evades us. No matter how fast we run, we never catch what we are after. Can you imagine chasing the wind, and how frustrating that would be?

After a lifetime of trying everything the world had to offer, Solomon finally concluded that the only thing that made any sense at all was God. He realized nobody can find any lasting enjoyment apart from Him. Solomon said what he had learned from all his searching was to:

Fear God [revere and worship Him, knowing that He is], and keep His commandments, for this is the whole of man [the full, original purpose of his creation, the object of God's providence, the root of character, the foundation of all happiness, the adjustment to all inharmonious circumstances and conditions under the sun] and the whole [duty] for every man. (Ecclesiastes 12:13)

WORLDLY ADVERTISING

Advertising is a major part of our culture. Taking a drive down the highway is like driving through an encyclopedia of information. In our everyday lives, we are bombarded with billboards, commercials on television and radio, advertisements in every magazine and newspaper and on the sides of taxis and buses. They all tell us in some way or another that we *need* what they are selling.

"Buy this cream, and your wrinkles will disappear." Isn't the message really that if you buy and use that particular product, then you will be acceptable? The message is that if you can just look better, people will approve of you.

"Drive this car, and you will definitely be noticed and admired."

"Spray on this perfume, and every man will be drawn to you."

"Eat this food, and you will be totally satisfied."

"Take this pill, and you will lose weight." After all, if you were just a bit smaller in size, you might not be rejected.

It is time to wake up! It is all a lie! There may be good products in the world that you will want to buy and try, but they definitely won't give you that final sense of fulfillment.

The world is deep in debt and going deeper all the time trying to buy what God offers for free: acceptance, love, approval, worth, value, peace, joy, fulfillment! The bigger house won't make you feel complete; you will just have more square footage to clean. The newer model car won't do it; you will just have bigger payments. The promotion at work is not the answer; you will just have more responsibility and probably be required to work longer hours. Oh yes, you may also make more money; but by the time you pay taxes and buy all the things you will need to maintain your new image, you won't have any of it left anyway.

> *The world is deep in debt and going deeper all the time.*

Go ahead and make a few laps around the racetrack of the world's system, and you will be saying with Solomon: "Vapor of vapors, futility of futilities, all is vanity!"

ACCEPT CHRIST

If you have never accepted Jesus Christ as your Savior, that is a good place to start. But even that won't fix everything in you and your life unless you also accept Him as your Lord.

I say about myself that for many years I had enough of Jesus to stay out of hell, but not enough to walk in victory. I took Him for my ticket to heaven, but I needed Him as my *all*. I thought I needed Jesus *plus* approval, money, position, things. Not so. Jesus intends to be everything to us. He does nothing halfway. He will never be satisfied with one little corner of our life. He wants the run of the entire house. As believers in Jesus, we are His home, and nothing should be off limits to Him.

It took me many long years of chasing after *things* to discover I had what I needed all along. I was complete in Jesus Christ (See Colossians 2:10). All I needed to do was believe it!

As I bring this book to a close, it is my desire to leave you feeling complete, satisfied, and fulfilled. I don't want you to feel empty and to continue looking for something to fill the emptiness that will only add to the pain you may already be experiencing.

You must know who you are in Jesus. You must understand your righteousness (your right standing with God) is found only in Christ. *Everything* you need is available for the taking. All you have to do is receive by faith what Jesus has already provided.

Let faith take the lead, and feelings will follow. First, you must believe that God loves you; you affirm it to yourself daily through meditating on it and speaking it. Your feelings will come along later. Start believing you have been made acceptable in Jesus. Ask Him for favor with the right people, and don't worry about all the others who don't seem to value you. They are missing out, because actually you are a great person, and a relationship with you is something to be greatly desired!

A CASE OF MISTAKEN IDENTITY

Years spent in an emotional prison of mental torment can result from a simple case of mistaken identity. I had an uncle who actually spent twenty years in prison for something he did not do. He was sentenced because of a case of mistaken identity. Imagine all that wasted time and potential!

Are you doing the same thing? If you don't know who you really are, the awesome person God created you to be, if you have a case of mistaken identity, you may let the world sentence you to isolation, fear, control and manipulation, self-rejection, and many other unpleasant things.

Our identity is established as a result of who and what we choose to identify with.

Our identity is established as a result of who and what we choose to identify with. The word *identify* means to establish the identity of and characteristics of something or someone by identification, especially in relation to others. If we identify with people and what they say about us, we will end up in trouble; but if we identify with Jesus and His opinion of us, we will no longer have an identity crisis.

The people Jesus dealt with asked Him Who He thought He was. They were furious because He claimed to be the Son of God. They accused Him of blasphemy. Jesus said He knew Who He was because He knew where He came from and where He was going:

Jesus answered, Even if I do testify on My own behalf, My testimony is true and reliable and valid, for I know where I came from and where I am going; but you do not know where I come from or where I am going. (John 8:14)

His confidence infuriated the people. He knew who He was (See John 8:12). No matter what people said about Jesus, He did not identify with it. He identified with what His heavenly Father said about Him. He identified with God!

Identification with Christ is a doctrinal foundation of the Christian faith. It is not taught as frequently and fully as it should be. Some religious organizations spend far too much time telling people what they need to do, and not enough time telling them who they are in Christ.

We need to be taught to identify with Jesus, not with people who reject us and judge us critically. You belong to God! Knowing that fact will give you confidence to walk in this world with your head held high. You will be able to follow your own heart and not be adversely affected when people don't agree with you or your choices.

From now on, when people say something unkind about you, respond by saying to yourself, or to them if appropriate, "I don't identify with that."

See yourself as complete in Christ. You will feel relaxed. You will be encouraged to press toward what you already know is yours, but in your pressing you won't feel pressured. If a person knows he has money in the bank, and he wishes to withdraw some of it, he gets into his car and presses toward the bank; he does not feel in the least bit pressured, because he already knows that what he needs is there and belongs to him.

If you can understand and believe what I am sharing, then you will stop feeling that you *need* something all the time. The longing in your heart will be satisfied with the knowledge that you already have acceptance from God. And most important, you will no longer *need* approval from people to feel whole. Approval addicts can only be set free from the need for approval by knowing that God already approves of them and by realizing that His approval makes them complete! We do not have to struggle to be right with people if we already know we are right with God. We know we need to grow and keep changing as God works in us, but we don't have to be upset about where we are now while we are making progress. As I always say, "I'm not where I need to be, but thank God I'm not where I used to be. I'm OK and I'm on my way!"

> *Jesus desires that you feel whole, complete, and satisfied.*

Jesus desires that you feel whole, complete, and satisfied. He does not want you to be tormented by the disapproval of people, but rather He wants you to rejoice in His approval. He loves you! You are a special, unique individual, and He has a wonderful plan for your life. Don't let people or the devil steal it from you. Look away from all that will distract you unto Jesus Who is the Author and Finisher of your faith (See Hebrews 12:2).

Meditate on your position in Christ according to God's Word, not according to what people think and say about you. Remember that people had terrible things to say about Jesus, and they rejected Him, yet the Bible says, "The stone which the builders rejected has become the chief cornerstone" (Psalm 118:22).

Many of my former critics have applied for jobs to work on my staff. One man actually said, "Had I known how your future was going to turn out, I would have treated you better when you were a nobody."

I believe God is doing something wonderful in you and will continue to do something wonderful through you. Your critics may live to see the day when they wish they had treated you better while you were still in the process of "becoming" all that God wants you to be.

Live to please God, not people. You have His approval, and that is all you really need!

Notes

Chapter 1

1. Confessing God's Word out loud will have a profound positive effect on your life. I recommend that you read my book entitled *The Secret Power of Confessing God's Word* (Nashville, TN: FaithWords, 2004).
2. John Maxwell's *Failing Forward* (Nashville, TN: Nelson Books, 2000), 53.

Chapter 4

1. Taken from various sources, including http://en.wikipedia.org/wiki/Kleenex.
2. Taken from various sources, including John Hull and Tim Elmore's *Pivotal Praying* (Nashville, TN: Nelson Books, 2002).

Chapter 6

1. Peter Evans, *The Mask Behind the Mask* (London: Frewin, 1969).

Chapter 7

1. J. John and Mark Stibbe, *A Barrel of Fun* (West Sussex, England: Monarch, 2004), 76–77.
2. Viktor E. Frankl, *Man's Search for Meaning* (New York: Washington Square Press, Simon & Schuster, 1963).

Chapter 8

1. Christine Caine's story used by permission. For the entire story, read her book *A Life Unleashed* (Nashville, TN: FaithWords, 2004).

2. Watchman Nee is quoted as saying, "Emotion may be denominated the most formidable enemy of the life of a spiritual Christian" (*The Spiritual Man* [New York: Christian Fellowship Publishers, Inc., 1968], 190–191).

Chapter 11

1. Zig Ziglar, *Over the Top* (Nashville, TN: Nelson Books, 1997).

Chapter 13

1. Corrie ten Boom, *Not Good If Detached* (Grand Rapids, MI: Revell, 1999).

About the Author

JOYCE MEYER is one of the world's leading practical Bible teachers. A #1 *New York Times* bestselling author, she has written more than seventy inspirational books, including *The Confident Woman*, *I Dare You*, the entire Battlefield of the Mind family of books, her first venture into fiction with *The Penny*, and many others. She has also released thousands of audio teachings as well as a complete video library. Joyce's *Enjoying Everyday Life*® radio and television programs are broadcast around the world, and she travels extensively conducting conferences. Joyce and her husband, Dave, are the parents of four grown children and make their home in St. Louis, Missouri.

Joyce Meyer Ministries
U.S. & Foreign Office Addresses

Joyce Meyer Ministries
P.O. Box 655
Fenton, MO 63026
USA
(636) 349-0303
www.joycemeyer.org

Joyce Meyer Ministries—Canada
Lambeth Box 1300
London, ON N6P 1T5
CANADA
1-800-727-9673

Joyce Meyer Ministries—Australia
Locked Bag 77
Mansfield Delivery Centre
Queensland 4122
AUSTRALIA
(07) 3349 1200

Joyce Meyer Ministries—England
P.O. Box 1549
Windsor SL4 1GT
UNITED KINGDOM
01753 831102

Joyce Meyer Ministries—South Africa
P.O. Box 5
Cape Town 8000
SOUTH AFRICA
(27) 21-701-1056

Other Books by Joyce Meyer

WHEN, GOD, WHEN?
WHY, GOD, WHY?
THE WORD, THE NAME, THE BLOOD
TELL THEM I LOVE THEM
PEACE
IF NOT FOR THE GRACE OF GOD *

JOYCE MEYER SPANISH TITLES

LAS SIETE COSAS QUE TE ROBAN EL GOZO (SEVEN THINGS
THAT STEAL YOUR JOY)
EMPEZANDO TU DIA BIEN (STARTING YOUR DAY RIGHT)

* STUDY GUIDE AVAILABLE FOR THIS TITLE.

BOOKS BY DAVE MEYER

LIFE LINES

COMING IN APRIL 2009!

We all have challenges or dreams that at times seem impossible. In NEVER GIVE UP!, Joyce Meyer provides a toolbox full of steps that will help you succeed in realizing your dreams. Packed with examples of people who relentlessly pursued their goals, the book profiles nearly fifty individuals who succeeded against all odds. From the builder of the Brooklyn Bridge to the mother who lost her only daughter at Virginia Tech, we meet people who have faced tragic circumstances and prevailed. Joyce reminds us that with God, nothing is impossible. By the time you finish reading, you'll want to revive your dream and start on the path for making it come true.